# BORROWERS OF THE NIGHT

This book is dedicated to the memory of
Elizabeth Rayner of Clifton (1812–1832)

O ill-starred wench! (William Shakespeare, *Othello*)

# BORROWERS
# OF THE NIGHT

## The Clifton Wood Murder

# Anna Best

First published in the United Kingdom in 2011 by
Bank House Books
PO Box 3
New Romney
TN29 9WJ  UK
www.bankhousebooks.com

British Library Cataloguing in Publication Data
A catalogue record for this book is available from the
British Library

ISBN 9781904408895

Typesetting and origination by Chandler Book Design
Printed by Lightning Source

# Contents

# Acknowledgements

This book could not have been written without the valuable contributions and assistance of many people. I would like to thank the following for their help:

**Family history:**

Margot Atherton; Helen Briggs; Clare Dooley; Geoff Hirst; Malise McGuire; Malcolm Rayner; Lucy Taylor; Elizabeth Whitmarsh

**Local history:**

Kai Roberts; Margaret Sharp

**Research and contacts assistance:**

Lauren Ambler; John Armitage; Garry Best; Helen Bramley; Martin Brook; Andrea Gibbins; Christiane Kroebel; Group Captain David Moss of the Worshipful Company of Curriers; Ruth Nottingham; Helen Roberts; Phil Roper; Paul Weatherhead

**Occupational information and expertise:**

Police Sergeant Mark Botham (North Yorkshire);
Dr Paul Sawczyn and Rosemary Sawczyn; Valerie Shelford;
Lynne Mackenzie

**Illustrations assistance:**

Dan Ambler; Alan Burnett; Peter Dawson; Derek Dick;
David Hemingway; Reverend Jayne Lee; David Mills; David
and Carol Whitehead; Elizabeth Whitmarsh

**Staff at the following:**

*Brighouse Echo*; Calderdale Archives; *Halifax Courier*; National
Archives at Kew; Wakefield Archives; Walsall Leather
Museum; Warrington Museum and Art Gallery; Whitby
Museum Library; Yorkshire Archaeological Society

Finally, I would like to thank Reuben Davison, Simon
Fletcher and Dave Randle of Bank House Books for their
help and support in bringing this book to fruition.

# Foreword

To attempt an investigation into an ancient, unsolved murder may seem doomed to certain failure. After all, witnesses cannot be questioned and there is no material evidence or crime scene to examine. So, although I had been intrigued by the Clifton Wood murder for many years and had carried out some research, I might never have carried out a deeper investigation had I not discovered that witness depositions given before the coroner had survived and were in the National Archives. I ordered them immediately. The content of these was so fascinating I had no option but to try and discover more – and was rewarded with a wealth of information, from historical documents to family histories.

As I studied the range of material more closely, a theory began to form about who murdered Elizabeth and why. This theory, while highly speculative, is nevertheless informed not only by the documents directly relating to the crime but also the social and economic conditions of the period.

Alongside the factual sections of the book, I have taken the liberty of supporting my theory through dramatic reconstructions, which, while entirely fictional, are influenced by the personality traits that characters revealed in the depositions.

You may come to an entirely different conclusion, of course . . .

# Characters

*These are the significant characters, and their ages on 31 December 1832.*

### Elizabeth's family – the Rayners

Elizabeth, 20
William, her father, 51
Betty, her mother, 46
Robert, eldest brother, 22
Sarah, sister, 26
Simeon, brother, 16
John, brother, 11

### Thomas Ramsden's family and employees

Thomas Ramsden, master currier, 32
Ann (née Brearley), his wife, 30
John Brearley, apprentice, 18
Joseph Stott, apprentice, 18
George Pratt, apprentice, 18
Rachel Brook, the Ramsdens' servant and Elizabeth's best friend, 17

### Others

Elizabeth Brook, Rachel's mother, Alms Houses resident, 51
Hannah Glover, Alms Houses resident, 51
Sir George Armytage, 4th Baronet Armytage of Kirklees (in Hartshead), magistrate, 71
Michael Stocks Junior, coroner, 33
Abigail Oldfield, the Rayners' neighbour, 59
Charles Ramsden, Clifton parish constable, 51
Samuel Brearley, friend of Simeon and John Rayner, 14
James Pease, innkeeper, the Black Horse Inn, 52
Reverend Thomas Atkinson, Vicar of St Peter's, Hartshead, 41

# Prologue

*New Year's Eve, Monday, 1832*

*In the hilltop village of Clifton, New Year's Eve 1832 is fine. As dusk falls, farm labourers, weavers, wire drawers and card setters put aside their tools and, in holiday mood, hurry to the Black Horse. Soon the inn is foggy with the smoke of clay pipes and rowdy with voices that brag, joke and gossip. Pints of beer are gulped down greedily, causing James Pease, the innkeeper, a deep feeling of satisfaction – this will be a profitable night.*

*He cannot know – has not the slightest presentiment – of the horror that the next day will bring to his door.*

CHAPTER 1

# Thou dirge of the dying year

This is the story of an unsolved killing.

On Saturday 5 January 1833 the cold facts of the Clifton Wood murder were revealed to readers of the *Halifax Guardian and Huddersfield and Bradford Advertiser*. In a short, unemotional paragraph it stated: 'On Tuesday afternoon Inst. an unmarried woman, about 20 years of age, named Elizabeth Rayner, was found in Clifton Wood, about 200 yards from her own residence, with her throat cut. She was last seen alive on the preceding evening and was in a state of pregnancy.' Suicide is delicately discounted by the journalist, who goes on to reveal: 'No weapon or instrument was found near her by which the wound could have been inflicted.' Yet surprisingly, the obvious alternative of murder is not mentioned at all; the report simply concludes: 'An inquest was held yesterday afternoon but the particulars have not transpired.'

After the coroner's inquest had given a verdict of 'Wilful murder by person or persons unknown', a second inquiry was held at the Armytage Arms. This was reported in the newspaper on 26 January, and in a brief paragraph the reporter informs readers that 'after a tedious enquiry, the evidence in many instances varying from depositions given before the coroner, we are sorry to report that no clue has been found as to the perpetrators'.

Later, due to the efforts of Sir George Armytage, the local magistrate, the reward for information was raised from £100 to £200 and advertised in the edition of 23 February. Despite the temptation

1

of this massive amount – using comparative earnings as a measure this was worth about £165,000 – the authorities never gathered sufficient evidence to arrest a suspect. The murderer – or murderers – got away with it.

Almost 180 years later, the case at first glance might appear not so much cold as frozen solid. Could another investigation possibly uncover anything new? I believe so. A fresh analysis of the witness depositions before the coroner, along with the knowledge of what happened to those witnesses in the years following the murder, give intriguing clues about who murdered Elizabeth Rayner, and why.

As in any investigation, we must begin with the discovery of the crime.

*    *    *

*It is Tuesday afternoon, New Year's Day 1833. Samuel Brearley, aged fourteen, is in Clifton Wood with two of his friends, Simeon and John Rayner, aged sixteen and eleven respectively. John is bragging about the rabbit he caught in a snare the previous day and his plans to try and take a deer.*

*'Not a chance!' mocks his brother. 'You couldn't hit a barn door at ten paces, you.'*

*'Shut your gob,' says John, cockily. 'I'm a tons better aim than thee.'*

*Always the peace maker, their friend Sam is anxious to prevent the brothers ending up in a scrap. 'Let's find out then,' he says.*

*He begins scanning the wood for likely targets. 'Let's see who can hit . . .' His words trail off as he catches sight of something a little way ahead. 'What's that?' he asks, pointing to what must surely be a bundle of rags.*

*Simeon, asserting his status as eldest, walks cautiously forward. His face drains to a sickening white. He gazes down at the body in its blood-soaked clothes – clothes he recognises. Transfixed by the horrific sight he mutters, 'It's our Liz.'*

*    *    *

At the inquest four days later, it was to Sam Brearley that the coroner turned for a description of the murder scene. It may be that Simeon and John, Elizabeth's brothers, were too traumatised to speak clearly of their grim discovery, or perhaps Samuel was a level-headed lad who could be relied upon to tell the tale plainly and calmly. Certainly his careful description of the body and its position suggests a boy of above average intelligence and observation skills. He recalls she was on her belly, 'arms crossed and her head was upon her arms'. The body was facing uphill. He notes the abundance of blood, some of it 'a yard above her in the wood', and 'some on her back, fair across her shoulders a great deal'. Other details are that her hair had fallen loose and her legs were bare, 'but her gown was not torn at the back – it was covered in blood'.

Samuel also had the presence of mind to check for footprints, but 'the ground was all leaves and I could not tell whether anybody else had been there. I could not see any footsteps.' Neither were there 'knife, scissors or razor'. His keen eye also noted how 'her shoe toes had gone right into the ground'. This, together with the blood a yard above her, suggests she was dragged further into the wood from the initial place of execution, presumably so her body would be less easily seen.

Whatever other thoughts tumbled through Sam's head, he wasted no time in alerting the village to their gruesome find: 'I came into town and told it directly.'

The suspicion of suicide seems to have occurred to him as instantly as it did to the news reporter – perhaps not surprising given Elizabeth's blossoming pregnancy and unmarried state – but clearly this possibility was very quickly dismissed because of the absence of a blade near the body. Even if a weapon had been found at the scene, it is unlikely anyone who knew Elizabeth would have believed she took her own life. By all accounts she had not been depressed in the slightest, her mood described by many witnesses as 'cheerful'.

But had someone else been far from cheerful about Elizabeth's pregnancy? And had that someone decided that neither the unborn child nor its mother would see the light of the New Year dawn?

The motive for murder can often be discovered through an examination of the victim's character, background and lifestyle. So what kind of young woman was Elizabeth Rayner? What kind of family did she come from? Who were the people she mixed with? By using a combination of official documents and oral family history, a picture of Elizabeth Rayner emerges that, while not a detailed portrait, is nevertheless far from the nebulous shade we might expect.

CHAPTER 2

# A branch of one of your antediluvian families

The surname Rayner has deep roots in the ancient parish of Hartshead-cum-Clifton. The first Rayner recorded there was one Reyner le Flemynge, who founded the Cistercian priory of Kirklees nine hundred years ago. A similarly grand connection is that in the sixteenth century the manor house, Clifton Hall, was the property of a William Rayner, remaining in the family for a hundred years. But by the time of Elizabeth's birth in 1812 her branch of the Rayners was an ordinary Clifton family, hard-working and settled in a small cottage on Well Lane – known in earlier times as Kirkgate, as it led over the fields to the church (kirk) of St Peter's at Hartshead.

William, Elizabeth's father, born in 1781, was a wire drawer. This was a dangerous but steady occupation. In Clifton it was a burgeoning trade, providing employment for many men, boys and occasionally women. The process required a rod of iron to be worked to a point at one end; next it was cleaned by being revolved in a cast-iron barrel filled with cold water. After this the wires were drawn on a series of blocks through holes of declining size until the required diameter was achieved. The drawn wire was then annealed in a furnace. Once it had been allowed to cool it was cleaned by immersion in vitriol. The wire could cause grave injuries if it snapped during the drawing process. There was a joke told at the time: 'How can you tell if someone is a wire drawer? Count their fingers.'

On 25 March 1804 William married Betty Chew of Birstall

(born in 1786) and soon children started to arrive. As was common at the time, two died in infancy – Annis, who survived only twenty-three weeks, and Mary Ann, who faltered yet sooner at just fifteen weeks. Even when those perilous infant years were past and the vigour of youth was achieved, death could, and frequently did, ambush the strongest and toughest. This was the case in the summer of 1830, when Crispin, the eldest son, died aged just twenty-one.

From a young age Crispin had been a lad of outstanding physical prowess, and by his late teens he was renowned locally for his feats of strength. Strong as a young bull, he must have seemed indestructible. Family history tells of him dragging a cart (average weight 18cwt) all the way up the sheer incline of Clifton Common for a bet. He made the most of his prodigious power by working as a circus strongman, bending metal bars with his bare hands and lifting loads beyond the means of normal men. Later he took the king's shilling, and owing to his impressive physique was made a grenadier. In the seventeenth century a grenadier guard was a specialised soldier whose fighting role was to lob grenades at the enemy and lead assault operations. Consequently they were chosen from the largest, strongest troops. By the nineteenth century, although throwing grenades was no longer an operational tactic, grenadiers were still chosen for their size and strength. As the awe-inspiring showpiece of the country's military machine, not only did they strike fear into the heart of the enemy but also carried out ceremonial duties, such as Trooping the Colour.

The story is told among Crispin's descendants of how, during a formal inspection by King William IV and Queen Adelaide, the queen stopped in front of Crispin and exclaimed, 'Why, you're a fine figure of a man!' to which he replied, without a shred of false modesty, 'I am that, Mrs Queen.' A larger than life figure, he was also Yorkshire through and through.

Why and how he died is not recorded or recalled, but the family's affection for him is illustrated by a telling fact: his sister Sarah named her second son Crispin in 1835, and his brother John bestowed the name on his first son in 1850. Perhaps they hoped their sons would inherit some of the attributes of their deceased, much-loved uncle.

Having Crispin on your side would have been like having your own personal minder, and although she did not know it, that is exactly what Elizabeth needed less than two years later. But why? What did she do to inspire such rage or fear in someone that he murdered her? To try and unravel the mystery we need to consider the victim more closely.

The facts about Elizabeth's life can be summed up briefly. She was born in 1812, and her baptism took place on 27 December in the picturesque church of St Peter's, Hartshead. In what seems an auspicious start, she was baptised by no less a minister than the Reverend Patrick Brontë, father of the writers Charlotte, Emily and Anne: at this time, however, only the eldest Brontë child, Maria, had been born. When William and Betty Rayner arrived at the church that winter's day with their infant daughter Elizabeth, she was the fourth of their surviving children: Sarah, born in 1806, Crispin in 1809 and Robert in 1810.

Although it can be difficult to be precise about ages before 1837, when an Act of Parliament made birth registration law, in the case of the Rayners we have at least documentary evidence of their baptismal dates, as these are recorded in the parish register. And while baptisms were not always performed in the year of birth, the spacing of the children suggests they were baptised near their birth dates, so that by the year 1832 the Rayner family were aged approximately as follows: parents – William, (fifty-one), Betty (forty-six), and their children – Sarah (twenty-six), Robert (twenty-two), Elizabeth (twenty), Simeon (sixteen), John (eleven), Edmund (four) and grandson Joseph (two), the son of Sarah, who is recorded in the parish register as a single woman by the letters SW in the column intended for the father's name.

By anyone's measure, a family of ten is a lot of mouths to feed, and there were times when the Rayners struggled to make ends meet. This is evidenced in Sir George Armytage's record book of rents, from 1816 to 1821, where we find William's arrears rose from £3 17s in 1816 to £11 19s in 1821. He was, however, not alone in owing substantial arrears, and the entries for many other cottagers and farmers follow a similar pattern. Sir George, it seems, was reluctant to evict tenants, fully understanding the difficulties they faced in eking out a living.

William was at least in full-time work, as was Robert, while Simeon and John were both old enough, by the standards of the time, to be earning, and were probably contributing in some small measure to the family's income. Work, although not well paid, was plentiful in the little villages of Hartshead and Clifton. A brief scan through the parish registers shows the prevalence of certain occupations: we find large numbers of wire drawers, card makers, curriers and farmers. There are also many people employed in various types of cloth production, such as croppers and weavers. Interspersed with these, we also find cordwainers (shoemakers,) joiners, masons, butchers and the like.

In addition to wages, some villagers would also have had the use of a strip of land to grow vegetables – although between 1770 and 1830 this useful source of food was declining as wealthy landowners exploited the enclosure acts to annex vast acres of common fields for their own use. If, therefore, the Rayners had a vegetable plot, they were among the more fortunate. Food accounted for around three-quarters of a man's wages, especially in 1829 and 1830 when bad harvests led to a massive rise in the price of bread, reducing many families to near starvation.

All in all, Elizabeth's background was in no way exceptional for her time and place: even her pregnancy, as we shall see later, was not of itself unusual for the period. On the surface, nothing suggests a reason for the tragic fate that was to befall her. Was it then something in Elizabeth herself that drew such malevolence towards her? Is there any way we can discover what she was like in appearance and character? The two sources open to us are the stories passed down the generations and the depositions given before the coroner.

According to family tradition she was a striking young woman with flame-red hair, yet without the stereotypical tempestuous temperament attributed to redheads. Indeed, the picture painted by witnesses before the coroner is of a friendly, optimistic young woman. We hear from her best friend, the servant girl Rachel Brook: 'She was a very cheerful girl and has never been low spirited about the child.' Rachel's mother, Elizabeth Brook, adds to this impression when she recalls that on the eve of the murder, 'The deceased was playing and very cheerful at Hannah Glover's.' Later in her statement she adds that her daughter's friend was 'a cheerful girl naturally. No one ever saw her low spirited.'

Nevertheless, this is not the whole story. The deposition of Elizabeth's mother, Betty Rayner, makes it clear she was used to more freedom than we might have expected in the 1830s. Whether Betty had too many domestic cares to worry about her youngest daughter, or whether Elizabeth simply refused to be ruled by her parents, the fact of the matter is that she came and went pretty much as she pleased. From her mother we hear: 'She has been out as late as twelve or one o'clock at night – she was mostly at Tom Ramsden's.' She had also stayed out the entire night on at least two occasions: 'She slept at Richard Walker's at Oakenshaw and the following night she slept at Tom Ramsden's – this was last Oakenshaw Fair.' Astonishingly, her mother admits, 'She never told me she was with child but I let her know we knew.' And as if this maternal ignorance were not bad enough, she also says, 'She did not tell me who by and I never asked her.' Betty also claims ignorance about her daughter's young man, saying, 'I don't know who she kept company with.'

The impression Betty Rayner's deposition gives is that the mother-daughter relationship was certainly not a close one, and it may be the family had simply accepted they had no control over their wayward daughter. Mrs Rayner does not seem to have been overly concerned when her daughter failed to return home by midnight on New Year's Eve, as she went to bed, leaving the door open. The next morning, apparently still not unduly worried, she did not start searching for Elizabeth until between eleven and midday. Although Betty's statement must have been driven by the coroner's questions and was possibly limited as a result, considering she is a bereaved mother it reveals little warmth towards her daughter or concern for her reputation.

Elizabeth's brother's deposition, on the other hand, shows a clear attempt to protect his sister's good name. Robert says, 'She had not been in the habit of staying out all night.' He does concede, though, that 'she has come as late as twelve o'clock'. He is also aware of her relationship with a young man called John Brearley: 'My sister had kept company with John Brearley, an apprentice with Thomas Ramsden of Clifton.' He adds that Brearley 'never came to our house and I never saw them together'.

The last point raises an obvious question: why did John Brearley never go to the Rayners' house? Was he not welcome or did he choose not to go there? Whatever the answer, there appears to have been an almost wilful blindness on the part of the family regarding Elizabeth's pregnancy and who was responsible for it. Robert echoes his mother's admission of ignorance with the remark 'I don't know who by and I never asked her.'

To summarise, then, the impression we gain of Elizabeth thus far is of a lively, high-spirited girl, taking her pleasures where she could find them; a girl who was viewed as cheerful and likable by those with whom she socialised, and who was dealing with her pregnancy in a positive way. The relationship with her mother can at best be described as distant, while that with her brother, although apparently warmer, is certainly not a confiding one.

But all in all, this was a girl no different to many of her class, time and place. Her pregnancy was doubtless a cause for gossip, but she was by no means the first young woman in the village (or her own family) to fall pregnant outside marriage. So what can this cheerful, ordinary young woman have done to arouse anger so violent that it resulted in her murder?

# CHAPTER 3

# See how love and murder will out

*Mid-afternoon, New Year's Day 1833*

*The festive holiday mood still rules the village. A few pennies have been won and lost over impossible, ridiculous bets, and the familiar old songs have been sung with sentimental relish and gusto, accompanied by fiddle and squeezebox. There will be more than the usual bleary eyes and banging heads tomorrow morning, but for the moment, ale flows in the Black Horse and the drinkers forget their woes.*

*But suddenly there is a commotion as a youth barges in. His face is a picture of childish fear: saucer eyes, pale face, breath coming in short staccato bursts. 'It's Liz!' he shouts, 'Liz Rayner's in t' wood! Somebody's cut her throat!' A second of stunned silence: then, as one, the drinkers surge out of the pub, following Sam Brearley to where Elizabeth's body lays, faithfully guarded by brothers Simeon and John.*

*In the little village of Clifton, New Year has arrived in the cruellest, bloodiest manner imaginable.*

\*     \*     \*

The 1831 census for Hartshead-cum-Clifton gives an overall parish population of 2,408. Many of that number lived in Hartshead village, others in out-of-the-way farmsteads or hamlets, so the number of adults in the village of Clifton itself would have been small enough for everyone to know everyone else. As news of the murder spread from cottage to cottage, many people would have stared in open-mouthed disbelief at the name of the victim. This was a lass who was very much one of their own – a familiar, youthful figure in their midst. The question on everyone's lips must have been who could have done such a thing? Surely not someone they knew. It would be up to the authorities to find out, and the authorities in 1832 were very different from now.

English law enforcement in the first few decades of the nineteenth century had more in common with Tudor times than today. The police force, as we know it, did not exist until 1856. Before this, the only policing most places had was the unpaid parish constable. Elected on a yearly basis and working in co-operation with the local magistrate and county coroner, the constable was a general law-keeper, whose main duty was preventing disorder in his township. His remit included the power of arrest and he could punish offenders by locking them in the stocks for safekeeping before presenting them to the magistrate. After this it was for the magistrate to decide what further steps, if any, should be taken.

A man by the name of Charles Ramsden was constable of Clifton at the time of the murder – his surname is one we shall meet again. Aged fifty-one, he was a farmer and a respected member of the community. It would have been his responsibility to examine the murder scene for clues, supervise the removal of the body from the wood and inform the magistrate, Sir George Armytage, and coroner, Michael Stocks Junior. Sir George would then have taken over management of the case, directing the constable to summon witnesses to the coroner's court and engage doctors to carry out a post-mortem examination of the body.

Aged seventy-one, Sir George may have been past his prime, but he was well equipped through experience and social position to direct the murder inquiry. As a young man he had studied at Oxford, graduating with an honorary Doctor of Civil Law, which may have been part of the reason why he was made High Sheriff of Yorkshire at the relatively young age of thirty. Two years later, in 1794, he was again active in promoting law and order (or some might say protecting the vested interests of the ruling class) by raising and commanding the Huddersfield Volunteer Militia to deal with food riots. These disturbances in the manufacturing centres of the country were caused by near starvation among the labouring poor in the depression that followed the Napoleonic wars.

In addition to his authority as a magistrate, Sir George wielded great power by dint of his aristocratic title, wealth and land. His full title, 4th Baronet Armytage of Kirklees (in Hartshead), county of York, was one he had held for almost fifty years. His wide-ranging business interests in mines, quarries and farming meant that a large proportion of the local population was beholden to him as his employees or as tenants of his cottages or farms, while yet others followed trades relying on his patronage. And if anyone should doubt he was a man of substance, they had only to look at his home, Kirklees Hall, a grand mansion set in beautiful parkland, where he lived with his second wife, Mary (née Bowles.)

Despite his wealth and status, Sir George was no stranger to tragedy. His first wife, Mary Harbord, daughter of the 1st Baron Suffield, had died in August 1790 aged just twenty-seven, only to be followed to the grave ten years later by their only child, George, a boy of twelve. The survival to adulthood of the two sons by his second wife would doubtless have been a comfort, but it is hard to imagine that he ever completely got over the loss of his first boy. Did the memory of that grief sharpen his sympathy for Elizabeth's parents, William and Betty? If so, it must also have sharpened his determination to bring her attacker to justice.

*     *     *

*It is nothing less than an outrage. Sir George strides along the path towards the stable block with increasing fury. What devil has dared commit murder on his land? And the victim a young woman, too. Too cruel, too brutal! Despite the biting pains in his joints, anger fires him with energy. He turns again to Constable Ramsden, who despite being his junior by two decades, is struggling to keep pace with him.*

*Charles Ramsden's expression is, however, as grimly determined as his superior's, and he listens with close attention as Sir George ticks off on his fingers the necessary tasks. 'Word of the murder must be sent to the coroner – that's Michael Stocks Junior. He's in Lord Street, Halifax. Tell him the court will sit on Friday.'*

*'What if he's not available on Friday?' asks the constable.*

*'This takes priority over anything else he may have arranged,' says Sir George in a tone that brooks no opposition.*

*The constable nods and scribbles the command into his notebook.*

*'We'll use the Black Horse,' continues Sir George, 'so let James*

*Pease know. And we'll need surgeons to examine the body. Summon Mr Hoyle of Mirfield – the man's a dithery old leech but no doubt his young colleague will accompany him, so that's two for the price of one. Let Pease know they'll be arriving this evening so the deceased must be laid out as appropriate. Have you got that, Constable?'*

*Ramsden nods. He has his orders – the inquiry has begun.*

CHAPTER 4

# Murder most foul

*Thursday, 3 January 1833*

*An icy January morning. A sliver of grey bisects earth and sky as a hushed sentinel of villagers line the street outside the Black Horse. All eyes are fastened on the small group that approaches from Well Lane. William and his son Robert bear Elizabeth's body inside the inn, followed by Betty, Sarah, Simeon and John. Moments later they reappear.*

*Neighbours and friends step forward with soft words of comfort and sad embraces. William's face is taut with grief and anger. It is not comfort he wants now but justice.*

*Inside the inn, the sombre atmosphere makes the high spirits of two days ago seem a world away. James Pease's servant girl stares at the covered body warily as she sets a candle nearby. James pats her arm in reassurance. They are awaiting the arrival of the doctors who will perform the post-mortem. Surely this will provide clues.*

\* \* \*

In the nineteenth century coroners' inquests were required by law to be held locally and in a public place: consequently, pubs were often requisitioned. Some were used so frequently that they even had a small mortuary attached to the building.

The date for the coroner's inquiry was set for Friday 4 January at the Black Horse, the surgeons arriving the day before to examine the body and file their report. Compared with the astonishing amount of evidence today's medical examiners can produce, their 1833 counterparts, surgeons Luke Hoyle and John Collings Leadbetter, both of Mirfield, appear little more than novices, their 'expert witness' conclusions striking the modern reader as those of the blindingly obvious.

Luke Hoyle was the senior of the two men, and the entire witness statement is given in the first person, although signed by both. His colleague may have been there solely as a peer for him to confer with, or it may have been Collings Leadbetter's task to confirm that correct procedure was followed.

Mr Hoyle's description of the injuries is brief. He deals first with the major one, noting a wound of about 2½in to 3in long across Elizabeth's throat. This he identifies as the cause of death: 'She died from suffocation of blood and the wound together.' He is unable, however, to deduce anything else from the cut, admitting, 'I cannot say by what sort of instrument it was done. I cannot say whether it was done with the right or left hand.'

Though at first this seems an unhelpful assessment, it proves interesting in one respect: it is the only piece of documentary evidence at odds with the account passed down through Elizabeth's descendants; for while the surgeon in his deposition states he cannot tell which hand the murderer favoured, oral history claims that the way the wound was made proved the murderer to be a left-handed butcher. We could, of course, dismiss this as nothing more than an embellishment to the story by over-imaginative descendants. However, as will later become apparent, there may be some significance attached to both the reference to 'left' and the occupation of butcher.

After dealing with the ultimate cause of death, the doctor draws attention to three other lesser injuries. Firstly, he remarks upon 'two abrasions of the skin about an inch long' which are 'under the left ear'. He suggests that these were caused by 'some rough instrument or falling upon a stone'. Next he mentions on the forefinger of the left hand 'a cut by a sharp instrument and the nail is black'. Injuries on victims' hands and arms are usually ascribed to defence wounds, and seem likely in this case. The final injury of the assault is recorded as 'a mark on the left cheek which shows blueish, as if a blow had been given'.

Although the results of the post-mortem are meagre, they do allow suppositions to be made about some aspects of the attack, the most important concerning the number of weapons used. Mr Hoyle is certain the cut to Elizabeth's forefinger was made by a sharp blade and yet cannot say what kind of implement cut her throat. Surely if it was the same blade as the one that cut her finger, he would have been able to tell. He also moots the suggestion that the bruises below her left ear could have been caused by 'some rough instrument', and while this is by no means certain, we are looking at a minimum of two weapons.

If, as it seems, more than one weapon was used, was there also more than one assailant? An attacker needs only one weapon to cause a fatal wound, so why take more? The most likely explanation for the different types of cut is that there was an accomplice. And if that is the case, the crime begins to take on the complexion of a cold, calculated conspiracy.

Considering all the injuries together, a speculative picture of the attack emerges as follows: one attacker approaches Elizabeth from the front and lashes out with a blow to the face, intended to stun or subdue her. Terrified, she turns and struggles to get away, only to discover her path blocked by the second assailant, who thrusts a knife towards her. She fends it off, but the point catches and slits her finger. Meanwhile, the first attacker grabs her and together with his accomplice, drags her into the wood, where one of them delivers the stroke that kills her. Although the cut is relatively small it severs an artery, causing blood to gush out. To avoid as much of the horrific liquid as they can, the assailants drag her rather than carry her deeper into the cover of the wood. Then they hurry off into the night to a pre-arranged place, change out of their blood-splattered clothes and dispose of them. The attack is swift, brutal and efficient. The murderers spend the remaining part of the evening establishing alibis.

The above scenario and variations on it must have rattled through the minds of many of Clifton's men and women, making rumour and speculation common currency. Every item of news would have been pounced upon, and by the time of the inquest much of the gossip would have trickled back to Sir George Armytage. Perhaps this is one reason why the inquest produced somewhat curious depositions.

CHAPTER 5

# She feared no danger

*Friday, 4 January 1833*

*The coroner, Michael Stocks Junior, arrives at the Black Horse in a smart barouche. He jumps down nimbly and makes his way straight inside, his clerk following at a respectful distance. He is conservatively but elegantly dressed, in dark formal frock coat and top hat. Aged thirty-three, Stocks has the confidence and authority of an experienced attorney.*

*Sir George Armytage, seated by the fire in the snug, looks up as Stocks enters. From behind the bar James Pease smiles wryly as he notes the split-second hesitation that precedes the men's handshake. Sir George is a dyed-in-the-wool Tory, while Stocks, son of the firebrand radical Michael Stocks Senior, is a Whig with radical sympathies. They are as opposed in their views as their privileged positions in society allow. For now, however, their enmity is put aside as they discuss the tragic case before them. Whatever their political colours may be, both are committed to uncovering the person or persons guilty of this brutal crime.*

*The clerk sets out paper and ink while Stocks consults the list of witnesses and jurors. The parish constable, Charles Ramsden, arrives now, on hand to ensure the attendance of each person called. He is neatly dressed in his Sunday clothes, but hopes the proceedings will not take too long as he needs to get back to his farm to attend to a sick heifer. He strides across the room to consult with coroner and magistrate in time to hear Stocks say, 'I follow your reasoning, Sir, but it's most irregular. What justification is there to call him, beyond what may be nothing more than malicious gossip?'*

*Sir George's irritation at this possible obstacle to his plans sends his blood pressure soaring. 'I know these people, Mr Stocks, and gossip it may be, but by God there will be a grain of truth in it somewhere. Besides, we are the court. No man here has the authority to gainsay us. It is our responsibility to reveal the truth, and the longer we leave off questioning them, the harder it'll be. You'd agree, wouldn't you?' he adds, looking to his constable for support. 'There's every reason to call them.'*

*'Them?' queries the constable nervously. 'Who do you mean, Sir George?'*

*'Why, Ramsden and his apprentices of course –'*

*Sir George has no sooner spoken the name than its utterance draws him up short. He glances sideways at Stocks, then both men look back at Charles Ramsden.*

*'A relative of yours, perhaps, Constable?' enquires Stocks, genially.*

*The constable looks a little uncomfortable. He, too, is aware of the gossip concerning Tom Ramsden's household. 'No, we're not related . . . at least, not closely.'*

*'No matter. But I think Sir George is right,' says Stocks thoughtfully. 'Let us see what the fellow's got to say for himself.'*

*     *     *

The coroner's clerk took down twelve witness depositions, which fall roughly into two groups. The first are the kind we would expect from a coroner's court; that is, they are from the people who saw Elizabeth on the evening she disappeared and help answer the main questions an inquest is tasked to discover, namely: Who was murdered? When? Where? How did the death occur? By what means did it occur?

The depositions in the second group, however, are in many respects unusual and raise some intriguing questions. Bearing in mind that it is up to the coroner to decide which witnesses should be called to give evidence and in what order they should appear, it is surprising to discover that the second witness was a man who claimed to have had only the remotest connection with Elizabeth Rayner, and no contact with her at all on the night she died. This man was Thomas Ramsden. And he was not the only member of his household to give a deposition: statements were also requested from his three apprentices and his servant girl, Rachel Brook.

We can immediately understand the reason for questioning his apprentice Joseph Stott – he was the last person to see her alive.

We can also see why the apprentice John Brearley was called – he was Elizabeth's young man. Rachel Brook, servant, is also someone we would expect to be called: she was Elizabeth's best friend. However, Thomas Ramsden, master currier, and George Pratt, apprentice currier, are at first glance surprising choices. We may assume, therefore, that some local knowledge was at work. Rumours regarding the Ramsden household, it seems, may already have bubbled back to Sir George.

As we shall see when we examine them in detail, the depositions given by Ramsden and his apprentices present a number of inconsistencies and raise numerous questions; but the story of events they set out for public consumption is basically as follows. After leaving his home at around half past seven, Thomas Ramsden spent all New Year's Eve drinking with friends in the neighbouring village of Brighouse. He arrived home at one o'clock in the morning. The apprentices, having spent the early evening together, separated at about nine o'clock: George Pratt went to Brighouse to meet friends; John Brearley spent some time with George Pratt's brothers, Joseph and Charles, and returned to Ramsden's by ten o'clock; while Joseph Stott, having accompanied John Brearley to the end of John Brodon's field between nine and ten past, went back to Ramsden's, and saw Elizabeth Rayner pass the Black Horse at ten past nine.

Before examining the depositions of the Ramsden household in detail, though, we need to examine the other statements for what they reveal about Elizabeth's movements on the evening she was killed.

\*    \*    \*

*New Year's Eve 1832*

*It is seven o'clock. Liz Rayner calls a cheerful farewell to her mother as she steps into Well Lane. She is going to the Alms Houses where Elizabeth Brook, the mother of her friend Rachel, lives: there is to be a party at cottage number three, Widow Glover's.*

*The arrangement to meet her friend Rachel was made the previous night, but when Liz arrives, Rachel's mother says her daughter is not yet back from her work at Thomas Ramsden's. Liz sits down to wait, but the sound of laughter from Glover's is too enticing for either woman to resist.*

*'She'll know where to find us,' says Elizabeth Brook. 'Come on, Liz.'*

*Inside Hannah Glover's cottage a group of young women has already assembled, and Ruth Glover, Hannah's daughter, is handing out glasses of home-brewed ale. As the party gets going the young women play traditional party games, such as blindy buff (a kind of blind man's buff) and thimble (where a brass thimble is hidden), and soon they are giddy with the silliness of their own antics. Elizabeth Brook is glad to see Liz is in high spirits, despite her pregnancy. As a single mother herself, she knows only too well how difficult the coming months and years may be for the lass. She wonders if John Brearley, the apprentice who has kept company with Liz for the last couple of years, will do the right thing by her. She is not hopeful.*

*   *   *

The Alms Houses were a row of five cottages on Common Side (now New Street), Clifton, owned by Sir George Armytage. Occupied by poor widows and unmarried mothers, the poverty of the residents is highlighted by the fact that both Elizabeth Brook and Widow Glover were poor enough to qualify for the Wheat Dole, a charity established by the Armytage family in the seventeenth century. The distribution of the dole was an annual event on St Thomas's Day (21 December), when the recipients were given wheat and either 6d or 1s. The record for 1834 shows that both women received one peck of wheat and 6d.

But what did living in the Alms Houses mean regarding the lifestyle of the residents? The picture the depositions evoke is certainly not one of puritanical abstinence. These may have been poor people but they were capable of having a good time, taking pleasure in get-togethers with friends and neighbours and making the most of holiday celebrations.

*   *   *

*At around nine o'clock there is a knock at the door: Liz's brother Robert has come seeking her. He claims their mother wants his sister to return home and help her. Liz is not convinced. She suspects that Robert, twenty-two and unmarried, is using the 'message' as an excuse to get into the company of the young women. Still, it may be true – and because she is by nature a helpful girl she decides to go home and see, but warns her brother jokingly that if he is pulling her leg she will give him a good hiding when she returns. As she leaves he jests she's far too little to harm him.*

\*     \*     \*

Within five minutes of Elizabeth leaving Widow Glover's, Robert also left. He says in his deposition: 'I left the Alms Houses in company with five young women and went on to Brighouse and it was twelve o'clock before I got home.' It is not clear from his statement whether the young women accompanied him all the way to Brighouse and spent the rest of the evening with him, or if he continued to Brighouse alone. What is clear, though, is the following admission about his message for Liz: 'My mother did not send me and I sent her home of myself.'

So was this just a typical big brother hoax, or was there a more sinister motive behind it? Whatever the case, it was the event that put his sister in harm's way.

CHAPTER 6

# A little one-eyed blinking sort of place

Clifton, meaning the settlement on the cliff, perches on a windswept ridge in the south Pennines, near the town of Brighouse, West Yorkshire. The Norse invaders who named it were clearly at home in its harsh environment and doggedly tamed the wild landscape, fashioning a patchwork of fields (folds) in which to grow crops and keep their sheep and cattle. Hartshead was known in earlier times as Herteshede, a name that means the hill of Heort. The two villages, geographically separated by Kirklees Hall and its surrounding estate, are known to have been coupled together as Hartshead-cum-Clifton as early as 1647. Before the nineteenth century both communities were predominantly rural, but by the 1830s farming was being overtaken by manufacturing industries, in Clifton particularly. This is not to say that a modern sensibility immediately took over from the old ways – numerous superstitions and beliefs continued as before. A prime example concerns the reputed tomb of Robin Hood, which lies in the grounds of Kirklees Hall. This, according to legend, is where Robin was interred after his kinswoman, the Prioress of Kirklees Priory, had cruelly bled him to death. There grew up a belief that stone chippings from the grave had the power to cure toothache, and the superstition was so firmly entrenched in the locality that eventually metal railings had to be erected around it to preserve it from further depredation. Another belief involved predicting which of the parish's inhabitants would die in the twelve months succeeding St Mark's Eve, 24 April. On that evening parishioners gathered in the church porch under the Saxon arch, as they believed that those predestined to die would appear and enter the church between 11pm and 1am. Did anyone notice the shade of Elizabeth Rayner enter on St Mark's Eve 1832?

Today much of the ancient landscape has been obliterated by new building developments, but the area of Clifton where Liz Rayner lived, loved and died retains its distinctive atmosphere. Some buildings may have disappeared, such as the Alms Houses, demolished in 1960, and the cottages in Well Lane where the Rayners lived, but there is sufficient period architecture remaining to evoke a bygone era. On Westgate stands the seventeenth-century Black Horse Inn, with its unruly jumble of added-on rooms; opposite is the impressive Woodhead, an ancient hall with fine black and white Tudor gable; and tumbling along the side of Town Gate a scattering of squat, crooked cottages borders the road.

Most atmospheric of all, however, is Clifton Wood, its branches and foliage overhanging the little stretch of lane leading from the Black Horse to where the Alms Houses stood. Once known by locals as Sheep Cote Lane (from the sheep pen used to detain stray sheep until their owners could retrieve them), this is the route Elizabeth Rayner would have taken between her home and the Alms Houses, a distance of around 200yds. Even today, with street lighting and houses along the side opposite the woods, this short stretch of lane is dark and forbidding. In the 1830s it would have been much darker and lonelier.

On 31 December 1832 the moon had just begun its waxing phase, producing enough light to aid an attacker but insufficient to make the crime highly visible. With easy accessibility to the wood through a gateway in the wall, and the height of the wall providing an obstacle to prying eyes, this would be an ideal place for an attacker to pounce upon his victim with minimum risk of discovery – particularly if there was a lookout in place. On a winter's night, once the victim had been dragged – or lured – into the wood, the high wall and trees would not only have screened the murder from passers-by but also would have helped to muffle any screams.

\*     \*     \*

*Around nine o'clock Liz arrives home to find her mother is at Abigail Oldfield's, a neighbour. Aged fifty-nine and a widow, Abigail suffers from poor health and the Rayner family do their best to look after her. Betty*

*Rayner often calls in with a small loaf of bread or a pot of soup, and most days Liz sets a fire for her, a task the arthritic neighbour struggles with: small kindnesses but they make the widow's life a lot easier.*

*Without knocking, Liz opens the door and walks in. 'Mam? Our Robert says you want me.'*

*Betty Rayner, who is making ready to leave, shakes her head and laughs shortly: 'He's having you on. I never said owt of the kind.'*

*Liz stamps her foot in mock anger and mimes throttling her brother. 'I could kill him!' She is not truly angry, but a little vexed at his practical joke.*

*'You'll never learn,' sighs Betty. Her tone, and the sharp glance to her daughter's stomach, imply a more serious subject, but Liz ignores it with a careless shrug.*

*At the door Betty looks disapprovingly at her daughter's hair, hung loose at her shoulders. 'Where's your comb?' she asks.*

*'I don't know. I think I've lost it.'*

*Betty looks at Abigail Oldfield and shakes her head in dismay. 'She's that careless!' And with this she leaves, unaware it is the last time she will see her daughter alive.*

*Liz is not at all concerned by her mother's comment and smiles conspiratorially at Widow Oldfield, who smiles back at her.*

*'Your mam lets your Robert get away with murder,' sympathises the old lady. 'More mischief in him than a barrel of monkeys. Never mind. Will you bide a while?'*

*'Best not. I said I'd go back if Mam didn't need me,' says Liz, eager to return to the party. 'I'll see you tomorrow, though.'*

*'Aye, God willing – oh, and happy New Year.'*

*'Happy New Year to you an' all,' laughs Liz, skipping lightly into Well Lane.*

\*    \*    \*

Every account of Elizabeth Rayner from friends and family remarks on her happy, carefree mood that evening. There is not the slightest hint from any witness that she believed herself threatened or in any kind of danger. Even the pregnancy does not appear to have disturbed her sunny outlook on life.

And so it was that at a few minutes after nine she set out to retrace her steps to the Alms Houses. She never arrived. But Widow Abigail Oldfield was not the last person to see her alive.

As Elizabeth made her way down Westgate she was seen by Joseph Stott, an eighteen-year-old apprentice currier, who, like John Brearley and George Pratt, was in the service of Thomas Ramsden. The Ramsden currying premises, outbuildings and home, stood opposite the Black Horse Inn. In his statement Joseph says: 'I was standing opposite this house [the Black Horse] Monday night, about ten past nine o'clock. Elizabeth Rayner, the deceased, passed close by me and I said to her, 'Hello, Elizabeth,' and she said, 'Hello, Joseph,' and went towards Sheep Cote Lane. She went by herself. I could see her go forwards about twenty yards. She answered me in good spirits.'

It is common knowledge that the last person to see a murder victim alive always comes under close scrutiny. Consequently, although Joseph Stott was not giving his evidence in a criminal court, we might expect much of his deposition to concentrate on putting himself in the clear. This is not the case. After describing his brief meeting with Elizabeth, he gives a garbled account of irrelevant events. He tells how she had come to visit the servant, Rachel Brook, at his master's house a week the previous Wednesday. Then he gives further apparently pointless information about his master's movements, saying that Thomas was not at home on Monday afternoon or on Tuesday. (We shall see more of this preoccupation with Ramsden's comings and goings from other witnesses.)

He next turns his attention to fellow apprentice John Brearley: 'I have heard John Brearley say that Elizabeth Rayner was with child by him. I never heard of its being any other person's.'

Finally he provides an alibi for John Brearley that covers some of the crucial period of the evening: 'John Brearley sleeps with me. He slept with me last Monday evening. He came inside at ten minutes before ten o'clock. I guess this and cannot tell to a minute or two. Brearley and me went to bed that night at ten minutes past ten.' Surely this is a peculiarly early night considering it was New Year's Eve and the succeeding day was a holiday?

It was common practice for apprentices to lodge at their master's house, and both John Brearley and Joseph Stott lived with the Ramsdens, dependent on them for clothing and bed and board. The sharing of a bed at that time was also common, because small houses often had to accommodate quite large groups of people. By 1832 they would have been apprenticed to Ramsden for four years, if, as was usual, their apprenticeship began at the age of fourteen. By this point the two young men were in all likelihood very close, their bond forged by working and living together. Was it a bond close enough to persuade Joseph Stott to lie for his friend?

Joseph's final comment has the effect of drawing attention back to Thomas Ramsden, whether intentionally or not: 'My master was not at home when I went to bed.'

To summarise then: Joseph's statement is entirely consistent with the type of information required during an inquest. However, it seems somewhat brief given he was the last person to see her alive. The paucity of information he gives regarding his own movements after seeing Elizabeth strongly suggests he was not questioned about them – at least not in any great detail. From this we can surmise two possibilities: either the coroner had information which put Joseph incontrovertibly above suspicion, or had much stronger suspicions concerning someone else.

# CHAPTER 7

# A policeman's lot is not
# a happy one

*4 January 1833*

*Charles Ramsden, parish constable, is not having an easy morning. Having already dealt with Sir George's gout-provoked irritability and Stocks's probing questions about who is related to whom, he approaches the workshop of Thomas Ramsden with an uneasy feeling. He has always admired his young relative: in fact, only a few months ago he recommended Thomas as highway surveyor for the parish, and a fine surveyor he makes too. And yet, already there is gossip . . .*

*He pauses at the gate to the yard. Ahead of him, just outside the workshop, Thomas is bent over a newly finished hide, examining it closely to ensure his apprentice has achieved the high standards he demands. There is something in the stance and muscled physique of the thirty-two-year-old that suggests the energy of a man driven by ambition. Charles can understand how this dynamic fellow must appeal to many women, and reasons it is not surprising he has garnered a reputation as a ladies' man. Even so, he reassures himself, that by itself means nothing.*

*He opens the gate and calls out sharply, 'Tom!'*

*Thomas looks up warily. As he recognises the parish constable, an unreadable expression passes briefly across his features. He strides towards Charles, smiling a welcome. 'What brings you here, then? Highway problems?'*

*'You're not telling me you can't guess?' exclaims Charles. 'One of your apprentices was walking out with her and another was the last to see her alive, and you wonder what I want?'*

*'Of course. Liz Rayner.'*

*The constable nods and adds drily, 'Aye. You might recall her.'*

*'Come off it. I hardly knew the lass,' says Thomas, a frown wrinkling his forehead. 'She were nowt to do with me.'*

*'Happen so, but they want a statement anyway. And they want John Brearley, George Pratt and Joseph Stott to attend as well. Oh, and Rachel Brook.'*

*Thomas Ramsden appears to consider what the constable says. 'Well, of course they'll want the lads, but why me? Like I said, there's nothing I can tell them. Rachel Brook doesn't work for me any more.'*

*'I'd heard rumours. Your wife not happy with her, they say.'*

*'Aye, well, you know what women are like. She convinced herself there was something going on. There wasn't, but . . .' His sentence hangs unfinished and a moment's awkward silence ensues.*

*'So we'll not have to drag you there in chains,' says the constable, his tone lighter now the unpleasant task is over.*

*Thomas snorts. 'No. It'll not come to that. When am I wanted?'*

*'Straight after dinner. You're second up.'*

*'Am I?' says Thomas, a nerve suddenly twitching in his cheek. 'Can't think what they expect to get from me.'*

*'Aye well . . . and you'd best bring the lads with you. We don't want them running off.'*

*Thomas watches the retreating figure of the constable until he turns down the lane out of sight. He picks up the sleeker that lies beside the finished hide and seems to weigh it in his hand before slipping it into his pocket. He must speak to the lads at once.*

\*       \*       \*

As with most rural occupations, currying was frequently passed on through families: Thomas's father, John Ramsden of Halifax, was a currier and Thomas's own sons, George, John and Charles, later followed their father into the craft. There is also evidence to suggest there was a tradition of currying among the Brearleys, his wife's side of the family. It is of interest to note that three Brearleys, who were transported to Australia for theft in the early nineteenth century, set up what became the biggest and most successful currying business in Geelong. Later, one of them became mayor, his eminence recognised in the naming of the Brearley terminal at Geelong's airport – a fine example of turning adversity into triumph.

Currying, as a separate and specialised craft in the production of leather, was a highly skilled and demanding trade until the early twentieth century, when it became absorbed into a mechanised system of manufacture. The fact that Thomas and his three apprentices were all able to sign their depositions themselves demonstrates it was a trade that recruited from better off families – families with the wherewithal to give their sons a basic education.

The craft concerned the stretching and finishing of tanned leather to make it supple and strong enough to be worked by a shoemaker or saddler. The work was tough manual labour, requiring a high level of skill and unique tools. First the hide was stretched on various frames, chosen according to the type of leather to be worked. After this came the hard physical stage, when it was scrubbed to soften it. Then, using a short bladed knife called a 'sleeker', the remaining tanning fluid was forced from the hide. The next stage was to dress the skin to make it smooth, waterproof, flexible and strong. A currying knife (also known as a shave) had a blade set at right angles to the handle, so it could be used like a wood plane to shave the skin's surface. This called for precision: if the cut was too steep it could make the hide worthless. Once he had trimmed the hide to the required size and thickness, the currier carried out the actual currying, massaging equal amounts of beef tallow and cod liver oil into the leather.

Thomas Ramsden, born in Halifax in 1800, was a master currier, having served a seven year apprenticeship into the 'art and mysterie' of the craft. By 1832 his workshop was a thriving concern, employing at least three apprentices.

Nevertheless, like many ambitious men before and since, he had a finger in other pies. He had already been appointed surveyor of the highways for the parish, an unpaid task and one that was generally unpopular, for it involved the surveyor compelling his neighbours to spend at least four days a year repairing the roads. He was obliged to report anyone who refused to carry out the duty. The post, however, offered certain advantages. Firstly, it was a position usually held by someone of high social standing, thus it enhanced Thomas's local prestige. Secondly, it put him in the company of wealthy men, such as Sir George Armytage, as it was a task of the office to present an account of the state of the roads to the justices of the peace three times a year. Networking, then as now, was a way to oil the wheels of business, and Thomas Ramsden was a man with an eye for the main chance. Finally, as highway surveyor he had the right to dig for gravel anywhere in the parish without needing permission. This was a considerable perk to Thomas because of his farming interests. He leased at least two fields in the Clifton area from Sir George Armytage – Wheat Royd, in the hamlet of Woolrow, and New England End, abutting Clifton Wood – and two farms, Low Farm and Upper Farm. Having control over the schedule of work for the highways and access to the means of repair meant that he could ensure the approaches to his businesses were well maintained and passable at all times.

As for his home life, at the time of Elizabeth Rayner's murder Thomas had four children living – George, born in 1823, Mary (1827), John (1830) and Sarah (1831). A fifth child, William Brearley Ramsden, born in 1825, had died several years before in 1827. His wife, Ann, was in the early stages of a further pregnancy, which would result in the birth of Charles later in 1833. In addition to his offspring, there were a minimum of four other adults in residence: at least two of his brothers (one is named in the depositions as Joseph, born in 1817 and so fifteen at the time); two apprentices, John Brearley and Joseph Stott; and possibly his sister Mary, born in 1802, who was certainly living with the family at the time of the 1841 census.

To all intents and purposes, here was a family man, ambitious and well regarded in his parish, whose knowledge of the murder victim was, by his own account, scant. So why was he called to give a deposition? Even stranger, why was he the second witness to speak? What information did the inquest expect to gain from Thomas Ramsden?

CHAPTER 8

# We are family

*4 January 1833*

*The kitchen of the Ramsden home is unusually quiet. Ann, Thomas's wife, concentrates fiercely on stirring a pot of stew, her knuckles showing white as she clutches the ladle. Slumped on a bench in the corner, John Brearley is idly whittling a stick, his long legs stretched out before him. The door opens and George Pratt, the apprentice who lives out, stomps in with a pail of milk. He lifts it onto the sturdy kitchen table and some of the liquid sloshes over the side, making a large white puddle that drips to the floor. John raises an eyebrow in expectation, and sure enough the storm breaks.*

'You gormless chump!' *shouts Ann.* 'Watch what you're doing.' *She snatches up a cloth and begins mopping the liquid while George watches, uncertain whether to try and help or retreat.* 'As if I haven't got enough to do,' *she mutters.* 'Just get out from under my feet. Go on. Out!' *she shouts.*

*At that moment her husband, followed like a shadow by Joseph Stott, enters the room. Thomas says nothing but gives Ann a look more meaningful than words. At once she falls quiet. He turns to the lads.* 'The constable's been round. Seems the coroner wants to hear from all of us. Today. After dinner.'

*John's sleepy eyes narrow at the news and his gaze seeks out Joseph, but his room-mate stares steadfastly at the floor.*

*George Pratt shrugs, then leans heavily against the wall, affecting a kind of sullen nonchalance.* 'So?'

'So you'll be there – all of you.'

*The command is met by heavy silence.*

*'What about Rachel Brook?' Ann almost spits out the name.*

*'What about her?'*

*Ann's voice drops to a low murmur. 'Are they wanting to hear what she's got to say?'*

*All eyes fix on Thomas. He nods. 'Aye. She'll be there.' He turns to Pratt. 'George, happen it'd be an idea if you seek her out.'*

*'Nay, it shouldn't be me that goes,' says George. 'She's nowt to me now.'*

*'I don't give a tinker's cuss what she is to you. Just do as I tell you,' says Ramsden testily.*

*Without another word George Pratt slinks out of the house.*

*'I'd keep a tight rein on that lad if I were you,' warns Ann. 'You need him on your side.'*

*Ramsden nods his agreement. It's times like this that remind him why he married her, and why he wants to keep her.*

*'Anyhow,' he says, turning to Brearley, 'a few things we need to discuss. You'd best be in on this an' all,' he adds, including Joseph.*

*He puts an arm around John's shoulders as they leave the house, and Joseph follows after. Ann watches them cross the yard to the gate. They are deep in conversation.*

\*     \*     \*

Samuel Brearley, John Brearley, Ann Brearley, Thomas Ramsden, Charles Ramsden: the repetition of these surnames raises an important aspect of the case – namely family relationships and the loyalties demanded by them. In a parish the age and size of Hartshead-cum-Clifton, centuries had seen the intermarriage of almost all local families at one time or another, and some families in particular seem to have developed exceedingly close ties. As a result, unravelling the degree of relationship between individuals is far from easy.

The briefest glance at the baptismal records of St Peter's, Hartshead, leaves no doubt as to the dominance of certain local families. These include the Rayners, Ramsdens, Brearleys, Stotts, Pratts, Brooks and Armytages – all abundantly represented. Particular surnames dominate each letter of the alphabet: for example, in the 1813–36 entries, out of 96 individuals with a surname beginning with the letter D, 47 were Drakes, 21 were Dixons and 11 were Durrans.

As a result, the relationships between many of these families are so complicated that they defy attempts to unravel them. Adding to the difficulty is the custom of recycling the same first names. In the Armytage Baronetcy, for example, George and John appear in almost every generation, and for the family historian this can easily lead to confusion. With less noble, less carefully documented families, certainty is often even harder to come by – or downright impossible.

The identity of Thomas's wife Ann is particularly problematic, as there are two possible candidates, born within a year of each other: one in Lightcliffe in 1803, daughter of James Brearley and Mary Ramsden; the other in Dewsbury in 1802, daughter of David Brearley and Susannah Gomersall. The Lightcliffe Ann is the likelier bet, given her mother's surname of Ramsden, but the fact that the marriage took place in Dewsbury gives the second Ann's case credibility, too. But whichever Ann it was, there is a strong indication of kinship before marriage.

This recurrent family link between Brearleys and Ramsdens is illustrated in the custom of including a mother's maiden name as a Christian name for one or more of a family's offspring. (There are many examples in the baptismal records of Hartshead church, such as Absalom Hargreaves Cordingley and Mary Hargreaves Cordingley.) Earlier, in 1797, in the Hartshead parish baptismal records we find a baby christened Hannah Ramsden Brearley. Ann, in her turn, named one of her sons William Brearley Ramsden.

Another strong indicator of family ties, as mentioned earlier, is the large number of Brearleys in the currying trade. One of these, a William Ramsden Brearley, stood as a marriage witness for Thomas and Ann in August 1822, thus providing further evidence of a kinship link. And was it a combination of family ties and currying that brought Thomas's father, John, to Clifton in the first place? While Thomas and all his brothers and sisters were baptised at Halifax parish church, the record for the final son in 1817 shows a major difference in that the father's dwelling place is now given as Clifton, not Halifax. There is a strong chance that John Ramsden may have been taken on by a Brearley relation, or perhaps he was given the nod that work in Clifton was more plentiful.

Turning now to John Brearley. In the 1851 census he gives his birthplace as Elland. An examination of the parish registers of St Mary's, Elland, records a John Brearley baptised on 29 January 1815 (probably born late 1814), the son of Benjamin Brearley, clothier.

The parish marriage records show that this same Benjamin Brearley married Mary Eastwood on 15 August 1814.

But how close a tie, if any, did John have with his employer's wife? Unfortunately there is no indisputable evidence of a family connection. However, one small piece of information does hint at it: the mother of Ann Brearley of Lightcliffe, Mary Ramsden, was also born in Elland, suggesting both families had branches there.

Finally there is good genealogical evidence to show that Samuel Brearley, the fourteen-year-old friend of Simeon and John Rayner, was distantly related to Ann Brearley as a third cousin once removed.

So what does the interconnectedness of the families prove? Perhaps nothing. And yet for many people in Clifton related to Ann, Thomas, John or all three, there must have been an understandable reluctance to suspect or blame one of their own for murder, especially that of a defenceless girl. Blood is, after all, thicker than water.

Baptismal entry for Elizabeth Rayner with the Reverend Patrick Brontë's signature. (Parish register of St Peter's Hartshead, courtesy of Wakefield Archives)

Baptismal font in use at the time of Elizabeth's baptism. (Author)

Detail of the old altar with Armytage family coat of arms. (Author)

Man drawing wire, *c.* 1900.
(By kind permission of Warrington Museum and Art Gallery)

St Peter's, Hartshead (Dan Ambler)

Well Lane, Clifton, where the Rayner family lived. (Drawing by Albert T. Pile for *Brighouse and Elland Echo*, 18 August 1950, courtesy of the *Brighouse Echo*)

Black Horse Inn, Clifton, 2010. (Author)

Looking down Westgate towards Clifton Wood and Sheep Cote Lane.
(Author)

Sheep Cote Lane, Clifton. (Author)

Footpath towards estate gate into wood. (Dan Ambler)

Estate gate into wood. (Author)

Clifton Wood. (Author)

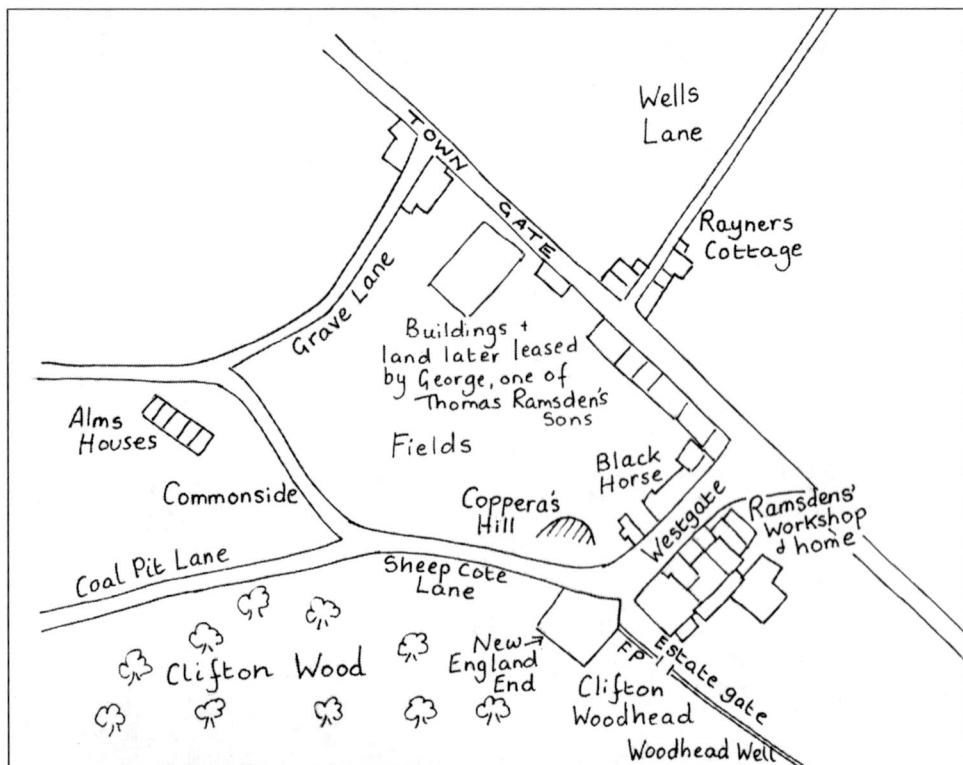

Sketch map of Clifton, showing
Elizabeth's route to the Alms Houses.
(Author's sketch)

Portrait of Sir George Armytage as a
young man. (From *The History of the
Armytage Family*, courtesy of the
Yorkshire Archaeological Society)

Kirklees Hall. (By kind permission of David and Carol Whitehead)

Kirklees Hall, showing eighteenth-century flying staircase designed by John Carr of York. (By kind permission of David and Carol Whitehead)

A curriers' workshop, 1912. (*Images of Ye Olde Woburn,* copyright permission sought)

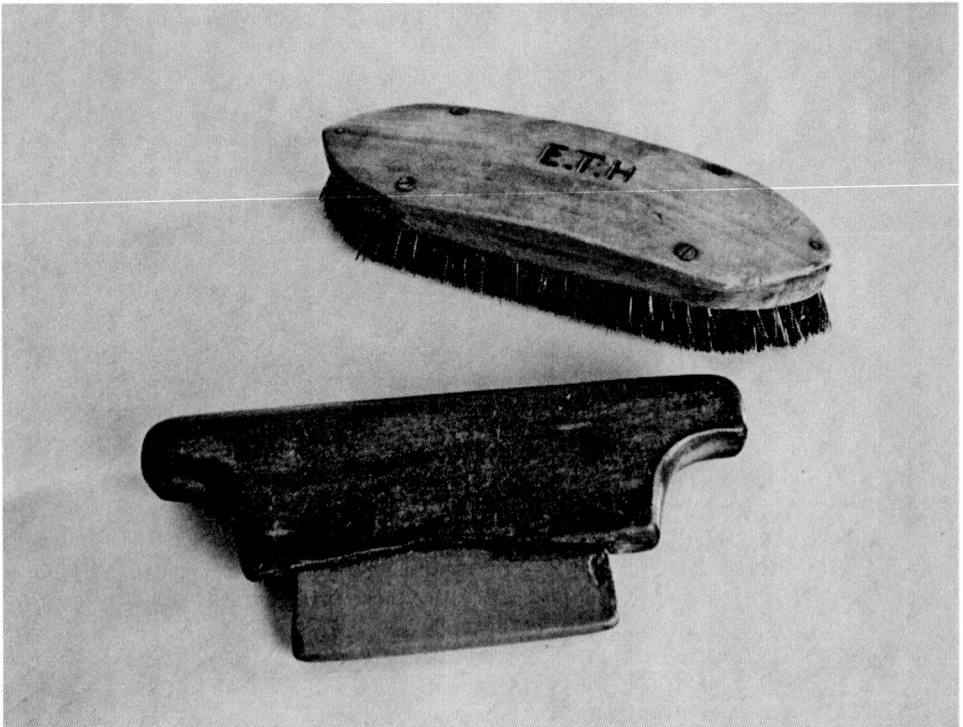

Curriers' tools: sleeker and brush for applying dubbin. (By kind permission of Walsall Leather Museum)

The Armytage Arms, Clifton, c. 1900. (Kindly lent by Elizabeth Whitmarsh)

The Anchor Inn, Brighouse, 1960s – now called The Bridge.
(By kind permission of Alan Burnett)

The Black Swan, Brighouse, 2010. (Author)

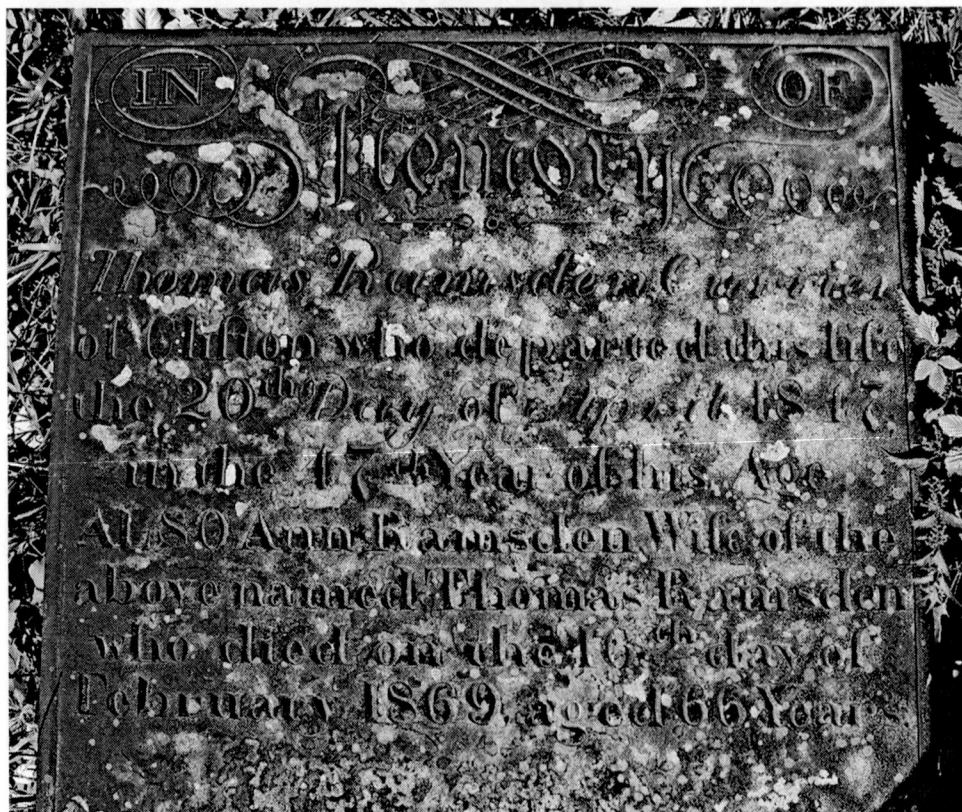

Thomas and Ann Ramsden's grave, St Peter's churchyard. (Dan Ambler)

Ancient yew tree in St Peter's graveyard, traditionally believed to have provided wood for Robin Hood's arrows. (Author)

Joseph Stott's daughter Nancy (middle row on the right) with her family. Her daughter Lily, the author's great-grandmother, is second from right on the back row. (Family collection)

Thomas Ramsden's son Charles (seated) with family outside the Armytage Arms, Clifton, 1880. (Kindly lent by Elizabeth Whitmarsh)

# CHAPTER 9

# Pitched past pitch of grief

*The Coroner's Court, 4 January 1833*

*The Black Horse is a heaving mass of people pushing and shoving each other to find somewhere to watch proceedings. Sir George beckons the clerk over: 'Tell Pease to shut the door. There's no more room . . .'*

*Suddenly there is a susurration of excited whispers as the witnesses file in and take their seats. Sir George glares at the gawping villagers and directs a sharp look at Michael Stocks, who takes this as his cue to start. He whispers an instruction to the clerk, who at once calls the first witness.*

*Young Samuel Brearley rises to his feet a little nervously, but swears his oath on the Bible with a clear voice. The gravity of his role as witness weighs heavily on him, but he is determined to recall events as clearly as he is able. Sir George nods with approval at the lad's sensible description of events. Occasionally Samuel glances over to where his friends, Simeon and John, sit in buttoned silence with their mother, father and sister Sarah. Despite the crush in the rest of the pub, around the Rayner family there seems to be an invisible force field keeping people away.*

*Michael Stocks questions the lad closely, but Sam needs little urging to recount his tale. Now and again Stocks halts him to ask for clarification. Samuel answers carefully. He feels important, unused to the rapt attention of so many people. Then suddenly it is over. The coroner dismisses him. He has done his best and is ushered out of the room.*

*By now the villagers are outraged by what they have heard, but wait with bated breath to see who will be called next. There is an audible gasp as the clerk reads out the name: 'Thomas Ramsden.' But before Thomas can rise to his feet, a bellowing roar erupts from the other end of the room. Liz's father is on his feet, his eyes bulging with fury, veins taut in his neck. He charges towards Ramsden, yelling incoherently, his arm drawn back ready to punch Thomas's face.*

*He does not reach his target. James Pease steps deftly in front of him, and with the skill born of years as an innkeeper grabs, then twists his arm, so he drops like a stone to the floor. Two more men rush to Pease's assistance, and despite William's frenzied struggling they hold him secure. Then, as suddenly as the storm of his anger had broken, it subsides, leaving him limp as a man made of rags.*

*Sir George takes charge. 'Are you his friends?' he asks the men holding William.*

*'Aye, Your Honour,' answers one.*

*'Then take him home and keep him there.'*

*William is escorted out. Thomas Ramsden straightens his leather jerkin, tilts up his chin and strides out to the desk where the clerk sits.*

\*     \*     \*

About two thirds of Thomas Ramsden's deposition concerns his movements on Monday 31 December. He documents his time quite precisely. He was at the Black Horse in the afternoon and left at about two o'clock to collect money as surveyor of the highways. This task completed, he returned to the Black Horse at about 7pm and had a gill of beer. At around 7.15 he went home to check on his apprentices, who appear to have been behaving with almost rustic innocence – George Pratt and John Brearley had been playing snatch apples, a game similar to apple bobbing except with apples hung on string. Thomas claims he left home at 7.30 and at around 8pm got to The Anchor in Brighouse, where he met George Widdop (also a currier), John Thompson and Samuel Lister. He claims he spent the whole evening with Lister, going with him to Mrs Waddington's pub, the Black Swan, at about eleven o'clock and staying there until somewhere between midnight and 1am. After that, 'I then came home by Clifton Common and down the town alone. I met no one.' He says he reached home at about 1am.

This narrative certainly has advantages: it puts him with a number of witnesses, and far enough away from the murder scene to remove him from the suspect list, Brighouse being about a mile from Clifton Wood. Although his recollection becomes vague after around midnight – perhaps he was the worse for drink by this time – and he reports seeing no one on his journey home, it is likely that Elizabeth was at least three hours dead by then, a point everyone must have realised quickly.

This brings us to the question of why Thomas was called to give a deposition in the first place if he did not see her on the night of her death. Was he a particular friend of hers, perhaps? Could he give some insight into her character or state of mind? According to the remainder of his deposition, he could not.

Thomas Ramsden is at pains to distance himself from the deceased. He states he knew her only slightly and saw her very rarely. He says that she was at his house the day but one after Christmas Day, but he only heard her and did not see her. He continues: 'She has not been at our house except the above day (and another when I was from home) for the last three months, during which time I have not seen her more than three or four times and not to hold conversation with her.' Right at the end of the statement he is emphatic: 'I never had any connection in my life with the deceased, indeed, nor did I ever ask her to have any.'

Bearing in mind Ramsden's claim of the most distant of relationships with the deceased, the beginning of his deposition contains a very curious admission. He says, 'The last time I saw Elizabeth Rayner was three weeks ago in Westgate in Clifton. I had some conversation with her. She came to tell me that Benjamin Glover was going to be married and he wished me to go.'

Why would Benjamin Glover send Elizabeth to invite Ramsden to his wedding? Elizabeth was a friend of the Glover family, true, but surely Benjamin himself would have asked Ramsden; they were, after all, close neighbours. Was it, perhaps, that Elizabeth was using the wedding as an excuse to talk to Ramsden – perhaps to get him to accompany her to it? Or had Ramsden been seen talking to her and wanted to explain away the conversation? But that aside, why is Thomas at such pains to deny any relationship with her? Is it a case of protesting too much? The clue to the truth of it may be in a further admission. Towards the end of his statement Thomas says, 'Rachel Brook left my employ on account of some jealousy of my wife that I was too free with her.' This unexpected and startling revelation immediately casts doubt on Ramsden's character.

Rachel Brook had lived with the Ramsdens for three or four years as a servant, so to confess before coroner and public that his wife had suspicions about his relationship with the girl was a certain route to censure and gossip. Considering how carefully stated the other aspects of his deposition are, we can only assume that his wife's jealousy of Rachel was common knowledge, and therefore he had nothing to lose by admitting it. An attempt at concealment, on the other hand, would have appeared deceitful.

Overall, the impression of Thomas Ramsden as a ladies' man comes across strongly. At thirty-two he was in his prime – a strong, successful man. If he enjoyed flirting with Rachel, perhaps was involved with her to some degree, then why not her friend too?

CHAPTER 10

# When lovely woman stoops to folly, and finds too late that men betray

*Rachel Brook is anxious. Hands clasped in her lap, woollen shawl wrapped tightly round her despite the heat of the crowded room, she sits huddled between her mother and Betty, Liz's mother. The image of her friend's blood-soaked body is still vivid in her mind's eye: it haunts her, turning every dream to a nightmare. Time and again she has asked herself if she was partly to blame. If she hadn't spent so much time playing blindy buff with the apprentices she would have finished her work sooner. And if the mistress hadn't insisted she finish the washing before she left, she would still have reached Hannah Glover's before nine o'clock. And if she had got there by nine, she would have gone with Liz when she went back home to see if her mother needed her. And if . . . Well, it is too late for ifs.*

*She stares intently at the floor as Thomas Ramsden gives his deposition, not wishing to listen but curious whether he will have the brass neck to say what every person in the room is thinking. So when he does, when he mentions his wife's jealousy of her, she feels a mix of elation and shame. There, he has said it, given voice to the whispered accusation; now she is free to speak of it too. She hopes Ann Ramsden suffers the humiliation sharply.*

\*     \*     \*

The first record of Rachel Brook (or Brooke with an e as it is written in the depositions) is her baptismal record from St Peter's, on 29 February 1816. From this we can assume she was just seventeen, or

43

almost seventeen, at the time of the coroner's inquiry. More telling than her age, however, is the blank where the father's name should be, signifying Rachel was illegitimate. Her mother, as noted previously, was dependent on the parish for poor relief, and this being the case it is likely the overseers of the poor had arranged for Rachel, from about the age of thirteen, to work as a domestic servant in the household of Thomas Ramsden.

Rachel was Liz Rayner's 'particular friend', and it is through her deposition, the longest of them all, that we find the most revealing information about the unrestricted social life she and Liz enjoyed, and their relationships with the young men of the village. With its strange blend of candour and concealment, her statement succeeds in drawing yet more attention to her master.

It begins innocuously enough. Rachel says the last time she saw Elizabeth Rayner was at Thomas Ramsden's on Sunday evening, 30 December. Elizabeth left at about ten o'clock. Rachel adds, 'She went away by herself. There were no young men in the house that night.' The words 'that night' seem to imply that this was an unusual occurrence. She does not say which young men she means, or where they had gone, but it is likely she is referring to the three apprentices and Thomas's brothers.

Moving on to the night of the murder, Rachel explains that she did not meet her friend at the Alms Houses as arranged, because she had not finished her work at Ramsden's and was 'washing and mangling clothes' until ten o'clock. 'When I left, all the family was in except Thomas Ramsden and John Brearley.' Thomas's brother (Joseph) and son (George) accompanied Rachel to the Alms Houses, and she 'went into the house directly'. Having seen her home, 'The lads went back. We neither heard nor passed anyone. I heard nothing in the wood as I passed on the lane.' (This was Sheep Cote Lane.)

Rachel mentions Thomas Ramsden again when she recalls that Elizabeth had slept with her a couple of times at Ramsden's, and then adds for no apparent reason that once, after being together at Oakenshaw Fair, 'Thomas Ramsden came home with us.' This flies in the face of Ramsden's attempt to persuade the jury that he had no more than a nodding acquaintance with Elizabeth.

Finally, although Ramsden has already mentioned his wife's jealousy, Rachel reminds the court of it: 'My Master and Mistress had some quarrels about me because it was reported he was too intimate with me.' In total, she mentions Thomas Ramsden (or Master, or

Ramsden's) thirteen times. If people did not already suspect him of having some involvement with the crime, they must surely have suspected it after Rachel's deposition.

The closeness of the bond between the two young women is commented on by Rachel's mother: 'My daughter Rachel and her were great friends. They were like sisters.' Elizabeth had also confided in Rachel the most about her pregnancy: 'The deceased told me frequently she was with child by John Brearley.' Rachel also reveals how far the pregnancy had progressed: 'She was fifteen or sixteen weeks gone.' Remarkably, she is the only witness who makes an outright expression of emotion about Elizabeth's death: 'When I heard Elizabeth was dead in the wood I screamed and went to her immediately.'

In view of her closeness to Elizabeth, it is perhaps surprising that John Brearley, the putative father of the baby, also confided in Rachel Brook. He had told her a few nights before that he was the father, 'but he also told me he had not got it all himself'. This phrase, recalled by other witnesses, is sly, suggesting not only that Brearley may not have been the father but also that Elizabeth had easy morals.

In defence of her friend's reputation, Rachel loyally asserts that 'I never heard Elizabeth kept company with anybody but John Brearley. They have been sweethearts for two or three years.' Perhaps she suddenly realised how this reflects badly on Brearley, for a couple of sentences later she springs to his defence: 'Brearley was very kind to Elizabeth and I never heard him say anything against her.'

Trying to be loyal to both Elizabeth and Brearley puts Rachel in a tricky position and undermines her credibility, particularly with regard to Brearley, for if he truly was kind and 'never said anything against her' he would have been more loyal in his deposition, and would not have suggested she was a woman of easy virtue.

The final person mentioned in Rachel's deposition is the third apprentice, George Pratt, who, she says, 'keeps company with me'. (George denies this in his own deposition, and we will examine their relationship in more detail in a later chapter.) It comes as a bolt from the blue, then, when near the end of her statement she tells the court about an apparent assault on Elizabeth by George: 'I never heard George Pratt say anything against Elizabeth Rayner – I remember Pratt nipping Elizabeth but I don't know the cause.'

This nipping incident is a peculiar and rather sinister event, also mentioned later by Hannah Glover, another Alms Houses resident.

She says the incident happened at her cottage 'five weeks ago this evening', and makes it clear that this was not just a playful pinch. George Pratt nipped Liz's left arm, making it turn 'black and yellow'. She remarks on Elizabeth's stubborn defiance, informing the court, 'But she did not call out.' Hannah's curiosity about the reason for the nip is keener than Rachel's: 'I asked him the day after why he had nipped her and he said it was nothing to me and abused me sadly.'

The most likely reason Rachel refers to the incident at all is that she was asked directly about it by the coroner. Perhaps gossip concerning the event was widespread in the village. But what impression does she give of it? First she appears to defend George, but closer examination shows her choice of words is slippery. 'I never heard George Pratt say anything against Elizabeth Rayner' does not preclude her from having heard from someone else that George had maligned Elizabeth. Then when she goes on to talk about the nipping she says she does not know why he did it. If she had wanted to turn suspicion away from George Pratt, she could have said the pinch had just been horseplay that got too rough. She makes no such claim, but like Hannah reports her friend's stubborn response to it: 'Elizabeth told me she would not have cried out if he had nipped the piece out.'

While not going so far as to make any accusations against Thomas Ramsden, John Brearley or George Pratt, Rachel gives a deposition that signals a host of suspicious points. She mentions Ramsden at every opportunity, she presents a contradictory portrait of Brearley, and she damns Pratt with a half-hearted defence.

If Rachel Brook was in possession of incriminating information, it would have been in her best interest to hold it close. After all, someone who had killed once would not think twice about killing again to keep himself from the hangman's rope.

*　　*　　*

*Rachel's tale is almost told. She notes the pitying expression in the coroner's eyes and it is almost too much for her to bear. A sob catches in her throat as she brings her witness statement to a close: 'She was a very cheerful girl, and has never been low spirited about the child.'*

*Rachel feels anger boil up inside her. That child will never now draw breath. She casts an angry glance to where Ramsden's wife sits, straight backed, hard eyed, brazening it out. There is a second of temptation – a second when she wants to scream out her anger, 'What was your part in all this, you scheming bitch?' But it passes.*

*She lowers herself slowly back into her seat, her hands coming to rest protectively on her small round belly. Rachel Brook is four and a half months gone. She has more than her friend's memory to consider.*

# CHAPTER 11

# Men love in haste, but they detest at leisure

John Brearley and George Pratt had much in common. Both born in 1814, John in the nearby village of Elland and George in Clifton, they were apprenticed as curriers to Thomas Ramsden. More importantly, both were having – or had had – close relationships with young women who were pregnant. There were, of course, also important differences.

John Brearley was very much part of the Ramsden household and, as already mentioned, was possibly related to Thomas's wife. In contrast there are no obvious kinship ties between George Pratt and the Ramsdens, and this may have been why he did not live with the family. Although he would have owed his master a certain loyalty on account of his apprentice status, it was not the more demanding loyalty of family. As a result this makes George something of an outsider in the Ramsden household and business. He was not, however, an outsider in the village: as fourth child of Joseph Pratt, a carpenter, he was a member of yet another populous and well-established local family. Two of his brothers, Joseph and Charles, are mentioned by John Brearley in his deposition; indeed they provide an alibi for him for crucial times.

\* \* \*

*John Brearley, his eyes set in a fixed, distant stare, can hardly believe it has come to this. He is standing in front of what feels like the whole village while whispers and murmurs of disapproval snake around his friends, neighbours and acquaintances. Making this statement about Liz Rayner is not easy. He is relieved her father has been removed, but is keenly aware of the family group sitting just within his peripheral vision. Why must they stare so accusingly and whisper to each other behind their hands? Even if they don't think he's the murderer, they think he's cruel to slander Liz's reputation. But how can a man be sure a child is his – especially with a girl as free in her manners as Liz was? What was it his master said? Keep as close to the truth as you can. Yes, that is what he will do.*

*     *     *

There is a defiant, somewhat sullen tone to John Brearley's deposition. In it we can almost visualise the resentful youth as he tries to refute accusations against him that are all the trickier for being largely oblique. His deposition is peppered with phrases beginning with denials such as 'I have never' or 'I did not'.

Perhaps the most chilling impression from his statement is that his relationship with Elizabeth, as he paints it, lacks any sign of warmth between them. This is most blatant in his description of what he claims was the last time he saw her, on the night before New Year's Eve. He was in company with George Pratt. He says: 'At Coppera's Hill we passed on the road but we did not speak. We were friendly for anything I knew – we frequently passed without speaking.' The phrase 'for anything I knew' is like the sulky shrug of a teenager trying to imply that something is unworthy of comment. But the more telling point is his assertion that they frequently passed without speaking. Is this the behaviour of sweethearts? Given that they had 'kept company' for over two years, this seems casual to the point of callous, especially when there was certainly a strong possibility that the child she was carrying was his. Contrary to what John claims, the incident suggests something significant. Adding further support to the suspicion of a rift between them, he says, 'I have been in Clifton Wood with Elizabeth Rayner two or three times but I have not been with her there since she was with child.'

With Rachel Brook's disclosure of his suspicions about the child's paternity still ringing in his ears, he attempts to defuse any bad impression she might have made of him. He claims he has never been out late at night and that he has never blamed a specific person for the child, although he concedes, 'I did say to Rachel Brook that I had not got all the child myself.' But Rachel is not the only person to state to the court John's suspicion that the child might not be his, so it would have been pointless for him to deny it: the frank admission makes a better impression.

Like Rachel Brook and Joseph Stott before him, John Brearley mentions Thomas Ramsden a number of times. The most interesting of these is near the start of his deposition when, referring to Elizabeth and Ramsden, he says: 'I have never said that my master had connection with her.' This statement cannot have come out of the blue – there must have been a reason for it. There are two possibilities: either he was questioned on the point by the coroner (in which case the coroner must have had prior knowledge about it) or he offered the information unprompted. If the question came from the coroner, we can assume someone outside the court proceedings had told him. If, however, Brearley made the statement unprompted, it may have been intended as much for Ramsden's ears as for the jury's. Alternatively, it might have been a devious way of putting the idea of a relationship between Elizabeth and Ramsden into people's minds, and two other points support this. Firstly, Brearley mentions that Elizabeth met him sometimes at his master's, thereby weakening Ramsden's claim to have barely known her and rarely seen her. Secondly, he boldly expresses her father's suspicions of who the murderers were: 'I went to see the deceased yesterday. I did not go before because William Rayner said it was all me or my master and he would have us taken up.' This forthright admission that her father suspects him or Ramsden at first seems so ingenuous that we are tempted to see it as an innocent man's comment. However, it is equally possible her father's allegations were so well known that there was nothing lost in referring to them. By bringing up the topic when Ramsden had ignored it, he makes his master appear the less trustworthy man.

There is a particularly interesting comparison to draw between John Brearley and George Pratt in the light of how they reacted when they heard Elizabeth's body had been found in the wood. Brearley says he was by Sam Clayton in Westgate with a music band when he heard the news. Nevertheless, he did not go into the wood because he 'did not like to see such a sight'. There are two ways the court could have read this. On the one hand they might have inferred that a man too sensitive to view his lover's corpse would also be too gentle to commit her murder. On the other hand, they might just as easily have viewed his reluctance to see her as unnatural and the sign of a guilty conscience. Surely the instinctive thing for most men on hearing that their beloved was murdered would be to go to her.

George Pratt was also nearby when he heard the news – in the Black Horse having a pint of ale. His reaction was the exact opposite. 'I ran down – she was laid on her belly with her arms folded under her head. There was blood around her neck. I came away directly. She was not turned over. She had not been touched up to that time.' Again there are two views that could be taken of this. It might be assumed that if he was innocent of the deed he would naturally be curious to see the crime scene – 'rubbernecking' is not a new phenomenon. Alternatively, if he was involved in the murder he might have been either excited at the discovery of it or anxious to see if any clues had been carelessly left behind.

* * *

*George has been left until last. He is not sure if this is a good or bad sign, but it has at least allowed him time to consider what the other witnesses have said. He fully expected the old hag Hannah Glover to blab about when he nipped Liz, but she has gone even further, describing how he had insulted her when she asked him why he had done it. The stupid old cow! She's made him look like an ignorant bully. He is in no doubt as to the impression her deposition made on the jury – the gasps, the muttering, the murmurs of disapproval. Well, he is certainly going to defend himself on that score.*

*He is also annoyed at Rachel's faint defence. She had promised to make light of the incident, but in the event has simply claimed ignorance. If she thinks he is going to accept paternity of the little bastard she is carrying, she can think again. And as if all this were not bad enough, he has doubts about the support of his master and his workmates. Their accounts of the evening seem remarkably clear – almost to the minute, as if rehearsed, and if **he** has noticed it he's sure the jury and spectators have noticed it too. He starts to wonder if he's being set up. Well, he'll give the court something to think about.*

* * *

George has no alternative but to speak about the nipping incident, and, as might be expected, plays it down. He tells the court it was something that happened about a month before at Hannah Glover's. As he puts it, 'I joked her she would not speak to me. I squeezed her a bit in my nonsense. I did nip her on the left arm but not violently.' As we know, Hannah's interpretation of the event puts a more serious slant on it. She tells how he made a bruise that went black and yellow, and was sufficiently disturbed to ask him to why. Far from obliging, he told her to mind her own business and insulted her. That it was Elizabeth's left arm George pinched may be significant. The surgeons' autopsy report says that the minor injuries she sustained in the murder were also on the left side – to her left cheek, left forefinger and beneath her left ear. This in itself is noteworthy – but there is another salient point to consider.

It is likely Elizabeth was attacked from the front: cutting a victim's throat from behind results in a much longer gash than the three inch wound she sustained. Therefore, in both the nipping incident and her murder, injuries on the left suggest a left-handed assailant, and this ties in neatly with the Rayner family's claim that the killer was left-handed. Of course, the Rayners also claimed the murderer was a butcher, yet no one of that occupation is mentioned in any documentation about the case. So is this simply wrong? Possibly. But there may be a simple explanation for how the error came about. Although a currier is certainly not a butcher, both occupations had to deal with dead animals. As we know, currying had declined almost to extinction by the early twentieth century and so as the story passed from generation to generation, perhaps someone substituted the defunct trade of currier with the more familiar one of butcher – a Chinese whisper of oral history. Consequently, how much suspicion does the left-hander theory heap on George Pratt? With only about ten percent of the population favouring their left hand, it must certainly nudge him further into the frame. But he may not have been the only character preferring left to right . . .

Returning now to George's statement, the most surprising revelation does not concern Elizabeth at all but Rachel Brook, for it is George who discloses Rachel is pregnant. He is the only person to mention it, and the way in which he does so once again draws Ramsden to the fore. He says, 'Rachel Brook said to me the last time she came to my Master's that I must have her child.' He continues, 'My Master and Mistress did not agree very well about Rachel as there was a deal of talk about her and my Master.' These two sentences warrant careful analysis.

Earlier in his deposition, George says he 'kept company with Rachel Brook over a year ago', putting the relationship firmly in the past and directly contradicting Rachel's claim: 'George Pratt keeps company with me.' Who is telling the truth?

It could be argued that Rachel would not press George to accept paternity without there being at least some possibility he had fathered her child, so perhaps the relationship had not ended as definitely as George says but had spluttered on with short reconciliations. However, if we look closely at how George relates this part of his testimony, a veiled suggestion becomes apparent. He says: 'Rachel Brooke said to me the last time she came to my Master's that I must have her child.' This is followed immediately with another reference to Ramsden: 'My Master and Mistress did not agree very well about Rachel as there was a deal of talk about her and my Master.' By mentioning the gossip and Ann Ramsden's jealousy of Rachel, he craftily plants a seed of suspicion that the real father may be Thomas Ramsden. If this were true, we can certainly see the advantage to Thomas of palming off Rachel and her child to his apprentice. Of course this would require George to acquiesce, and as we shall see from the next part of his deposition he was in no mood to be compliant.

George goes on to undermine the credibility of Ramsden – and Brearley – when he takes issue with some of their evidence about the early part of New Year's Eve. Thomas says that when he got home at 7.15, Pratt and Brearley had been playing snatch apples. John Brearley's statement agrees with this: 'We played at blindy buff during the evening for some time before milking time and after that at snatch apples.' George Pratt begs to differ and states, 'We did not play at any other games than blindy buff at my Master's.' This emphatic denial of what appears to be a mundane point may be a quiet threat to Ramsden that he cannot take George's co-operation for granted.

Another way to account for the difference in their statements could be that as a non-resident at Ramsden's he had not been as thoroughly briefed about what to say as Brearley and Stott. However, the strong emphasis of 'we did not play any other games' seems intended to make a point.

One other notable aspect of George's deposition is the way he concludes it. Having told the coroner he has heard Brearley say someone joined him at the child, he adds, 'I have seen Walsh's lad with her at the wood end.' As this is the only reference to Walsh's lad, and as the individual was not called to give a deposition, we can assume the authorities were confident he had no involvement in the murder. So why did George say it? He may simply have been mistaken: he may indeed have seen Elizabeth at the wood end with Walsh's lad, but it could have been a totally innocent friendship. A second possibility is that he might have felt he had gone too far in undermining the credibility of Ramsden and Brearley, so the story of Walsh's lad is an attempt to lay a false trail. By introducing another name he not only lengthens the list of suspects but also sullies Elizabeth's reputation even further.

The overall impression is that George Pratt's and John Brearley's depositions are webs of truths, half truths and outright lies. Of course they were not alone in this.

# CHAPTER 12

# T'ain't what you say, it's the way that you say it

The jury in the coroner's court came to the expected verdict: wilful murder by person or persons unknown.

*     *     *

*As the Black Horse empties, James Pease pours a glass of port for Michael Stocks and one of Madeira for Sir George.*

*'What's your impression, then?' Sir George asks Stocks.*

*Stocks takes a thoughtful sip from his glass, then returns it slowly to the table. 'They're lying,' he says.*

*'Of course they're lying!' exclaims Sir George, rolling his eyes in cartoonish exasperation. 'At least, some of them are . . . but which ones, sir? Can you divine a man's heart in his face, eh?'*

*Sir George fancies himself a master in the art of detecting the criminal from clues of physiognomy and bearing. Why, only five years before he had known at a glance which of the poachers charged with the murder of his game warden were the ringleaders. He had been proved correct: Isaiah and Joseph Bentley, and several of their fellow thugs, had reaped the whirlwind – transportation beyond the seas for seven years. In Sir George's opinion they were fortunate not to have swung for it. As for the present case, he already believes he knows who is pulling the strings.*

*Michael Stocks Junior has enough experience by now to know that the guilty often walk free. He knows as well that all too often the innocent are charged and punished. 'I have my theories of course,' he says. 'But theories alone aren't sufficient to clap a man in leg-irons. I fear this case may go unsolved.'*

*'Nonsense! The depositions are as full of holes as a sieve. And you marked the outburst of William Rayner, the father?'*

*'Of course. I was of a mind to call him up to testify but . . .'*

*'The man's half mad with grief,' interrupts Sir George. 'Reckless words with no more substance than tittle-tattle. It wouldn't have helped the case. Besides, I'll wager we can prise a tongue loose from someone. A reward of say . . . £100 should suffice.'*

*Stocks's expression suggests doubt. 'Can such a large amount be raised?'*

*'It most certainly can,' replies Sir George. 'I'll take charge of the matter. Where I lead, others will follow. I'll have the vicar make an announcement on Sunday morning. They're burying her the day after tomorrow, so people will want to express their condolences. The best way to do that is a monetary contribution. In the meantime, we must look to setting another hearing.'*

*'Here?'*

*'No. The Armytage Arms will suit us better. I'll send you word of the arrangements.' Suddenly Sir George feels many of his seventy-one years slip away. He is invigorated by the challenge ahead and rubs his hands together like a man about to heft a shovel.*

*Stocks pulls on his coat and places his top hat on his head at a somewhat jaunty angle. 'In the meantime, it might be wise to ask your constable to make some discreet enquiries,' he says.*

*'Enquiries yes, discreet no. My constable is a man of the blunt persuasion. But I guarantee you this: Tom Ramsden and his lads will be shaking in their boots once they hear we're pursuing this matter. And they will be right to shake.'*

\*     \*     \*

The initial outlook for solving the murder must have appeared bright. After all, in a small and tightly knit community everyone knows everyone else's business, and the gossip, wild as it may be, often carries a kernel of truth. However, that same web of communication can also imprison truth. The veiled threat of 'I know where you live' rings frighteningly close in a small village.

Sir George's confidence was ill placed. Despite the lure of the money, no one came forward with information and without the help of an informer the authorities were left with only the depositions and the prospect of a future inquiry to aid them. Poring over accounts from the witnesses, it is certain they will have focused on two aspects: opportunity and motive.

By and large, accounts of Elizabeth's movements on the evening of her murder, up to her leaving her neighbour Abigail Oldfield's, seem reliable and honest. They are presented by people who had nothing to gain from her death and are corroborated by other witnesses, while the times, though approximate, tie in with the distances between the various locations. We may include her mother's in this set of statements, along with Elizabeth Brook's, Widow Hannah Glover's and Widow Abigail Oldfield's. Her brother Robert's deposition can, on the whole, be trusted too, because although the joke he played on her appears suspicious in hindsight, his jaunt to Brighouse in the company of five young women gives him a sure alibi if we accept that the murder happened at about 9.10pm.

To recap then, Abigail Oldfield says Elizabeth left her house some minutes after 9pm to return to the Alms Houses. Joseph Stott reports that she passed him as he stood opposite the Black Horse at about 9.10, which means she had a distance of no more than 100yds left to travel along Sheep Cote Lane – a distance that should have taken no more than a couple of minutes. Given that she never arrived back at the Alms Houses, the most likely explanation is that she met her death shortly after this last sighting.

Returning to the statements of Thomas Ramsden and his apprentices, we have already noted their odd mixture of vagueness and accuracy, revelation and concealment, confirmation and contradiction, and this extends to how they account for their movements on New Year's Eve. Ramsden's statement is by far the most coherent. We can imagine him answering the coroner's questions in a forthright manner, not pausing to wait for the next one but pressing on with what he wants to say. Thus he presents the information about his movements in a chronological and rational way. Nevertheless, he takes the first opportunity offered to make a vigorous denial of any relationship with Elizabeth Rayner, stating right from the start, and with some force, that he barely knew her. Next he gives details of his whereabouts on New Year's Eve. He is very clear about where he was and when, and has three witnesses – John Thompson, George Widdop and Samuel Lister – who can place him over a mile away, at The Anchor in Brighouse, at the probable time of the murder. Of his three companions that evening, we know that at least two had sufficiently thriving businesses to appear in *Piggot's Trade Directory* for the area of Rastrick and Brighouse with Hipperholme: George Widdop as a currier and Samuel Lister as a shopkeeper. These were men of above average status who would guard their reputations jealously. By spending the evening with them, Thomas Ramsden ensured he had a strong alibi. Thomas says the four of them stayed at The Anchor until after midnight, their evening out concluding at the Black Swan at some time between midnight and 1am – presumably at about 12.30am, as he had said earlier in the statement that he was home at around one o'clock. He tells the court he slept at home that night, implying that this was not always the case, and got up at eight o'clock the next morning. His statement concludes with the admission that there was discord between him and his wife because of his attentions to Rachel Brook, but he strongly denies having, or ever having sought, any connection with Elizabeth Rayner.

The apprentices' statements by comparison, are almost stream of consciousness. They jump from topic to topic with alarming disregard for a coherent narrative. It may be that this was owing to how they were questioned, but given that Michael Stocks was an experienced coroner and Ramsden manages to present a fairly logical statement, it seems more likely they were nervous and unsure of themselves.

Joseph Stott's is the briefest and most enigmatic deposition. It seems the coroner does not have much interest in him, apart from his sighting of Elizabeth outside the Black Horse. And why would Joseph excite much interest? He is rarely mentioned by the other witnesses and had not had a close relationship with either Elizabeth or Rachel. He arouses so little interest that he almost slips beneath the radar. And yet . . . Joseph Stott was the last person to see Elizabeth alive – but he gives no account of where he was between seeing her outside the Black Horse at ten past nine and about five to ten, when he claims John Brearley arrived home – a good fifty minute period. It may be that he went straight back to Ramsden's and was seen there by the rest of the Ramsden household. If this was the case, he would know he had nothing to worry about regarding an alibi. Rachel Brook says that when she left at about ten 'all the family were in except Thomas Ramsden and John Brearley'. Nevertheless, we do not know *exactly* what time Stott arrived.

Joseph says nothing about events earlier in the evening of 31

December. Unlike the other apprentices and his master, he does not mention games or milking. He does not refer to George Pratt at all and speaks of his master only to say he was 'not at home on Monday afternoon nor on Tuesday' and 'was not at home when I went to bed'. He speaks mostly of John Brearley, saying his friend had told him that 'Elizabeth Rayner was with child by him'. Most importantly, he says that John Brearley got home at about ten to ten and the two of them went to bed at ten past ten. The brevity of the statement could mean Stott was a young man of few words with little evidence to give, or alternatively he did not trust himself to say much.

John Brearley, on the other hand, has a lot to say. He begins his statement in an organised, coherent manner, but this is not sustained. After describing his relationship with Elizabeth, he moves quickly to an explanation of where he was and what he was doing in the period from nine o'clock, when he left his master's, to going to bed at ten past ten. Was this because he knew it was the crucial time period? And yet there is a glaring omission. Rachel Brook says he went out of the house at 7.30, at about the same time Ramsden set off for Brighouse, but this is not mentioned by any other witness. While we know Elizabeth was alive until at least ten past nine, could the departure of Ramsden and Brearley together have been to allow them to talk privately – to confirm their plans?

After this section of evidence John becomes erratic, jumping from topic to topic. This may be down to the coroner's questioning technique, or it may be that the earlier part of his statement is carefully rehearsed, dealing as it does with the most significant parts. Once this is out of the way, his testimony loses the coherence careful preparation gives. He does, however, counter Rachel's statement that he was not home when she left Ramsden's at about ten o'clock, by claiming she had left before ten. The time line is a fine one and, of course, they could have missed each other by seconds, but it is telling how John is quick to correct her.

George Pratt's deposition is in very obvious contrast to Brearley's. Where Brearley is specific about times, George is on occasion vague in the extreme. At one point he says, 'I had seen my master about three o'clock that afternoon. I cannot say whether it was morning or the afternoon.' Is this the confusion of someone who has not really thought about their movements, or is it someone who has not been fully primed about what to say and as a result is deliberately vague?

George Pratt does not speak of anyone accompanying him on

his journey to Brighouse, but does talk about walking home with two friends – James Crabtree and Joseph Hirst. Given that the period in which Elizabeth was most likely murdered was probably a little after ten past nine, it would follow that this is the part of the evening the murderer would take care to account for. George seems unaware of this as a crucial time, and so blithely leaves himself without anyone to provide him with an alibi. Therefore if he was of an anxious disposition or a suspicious nature, he might have been feeling a little uneasy by the end of the coroner's session. He might have noticed that Brearley has an alibi from Joseph Stott and also his own brothers, Joseph and Charles Pratt; Stott has one from Brearley for up to ten past nine and the Ramsden household afterwards; and Ramsden has Lister, Widdop and Thompson for the majority of the evening. Could this be another reason George feels it necessary to widen the list of suspects, by claiming he saw Elizabeth with Walsh's lad at the wood head?

Considering opportunity, then, only Thomas Ramsden (physically at least) is in the clear. Elizabeth was certainly alive up to ten past nine, by which time Ramsden was at a busy public house with three respectable friends. The apprentices, though, were literally within striking distance.

A closer look at their statements raises a number of questions. The three young men claim they came out of Ramsden's at about five to nine. About fifteen minutes later Joseph Stott says he was standing opposite the Black Horse when Elizabeth passed him. But why was he standing there a good ten minutes after separating from Brearley and Pratt? Why had he not gone straight back into Ramsden's? Could it be that he was the lookout, ready to signal when Elizabeth was coming and if the coast was clear for an accomplice to grab her?

John Brearley says that on leaving Ramsden's he walked with Joseph Stott to the end of John Brodon's field, and then went into Joseph Pratt's until half past nine. But why spend the evening with George's brothers and not George, his workmate? What if, rather than going straight to Joseph Pratt's, he hid in the shadows near the entrance to the wood, ready to drag Elizabeth in?

George Pratt says he went to Brighouse when he left Ramsden's, but does not mention anyone accompanying him there. What if he did not go straight to Brighouse? What if he took up position further along Sheep Cote Lane, ready to accost Elizabeth or prevent her escape?

Of course the time available to carry out the murder was limited.

There would have been a great deal of blood, some of which would certainly have covered the clothing of the murderer or murderers. But if this was a planned attack they would be prepared. There is a well near the wood which they could have used to wash themselves. They would have had another set of clothes to change into. One of the lads, probably Stott, could have taken the soiled clothes away and disposed of them, and then returned to Ramsden's, carrying out tasks in the stable or mistal (cowshed) while Pratt and Brearley made sure they were far from each other and with other friends for the evening. So far, so possible. But we are still faced with the big question: why?

We must now turn to motive.

# CHAPTER 13

# It is a wise father that knows its child

*6 January 1833*

*The churchyard of St Peter's is strafed by a biting wind from the north east. Rachel stands close by the old blasted yew tree for shelter. She recalls telling Liz that Robin Hood used the wood of this very tree to fashion his arrows from.*

*'More use to me if it had been Cupid!' Liz had joked.*

*Funny how people thought love hit you like an arrow. Shouldn't it be hate that worked that way? Of course people killed for love sometimes, didn't they? Sometimes the rival simply had to be removed. And, to be honest, if she had the opportunity and the means Ramsden's wife would not be long for this world.*

*Rachel screws her eyes up against the wind and scans the distance. Yes, there it is. The funeral procession is approaching across the field, a huge crowd following the coffin. Well, Liz set their tongues wagging more than a few times in life; she would laugh herself daft to see them all trooping along in such solemn quiet to see her off.*

*The baby inside her makes a sharp, sudden movement. Her hand flies instinctively to her stomach and strokes it, as if she is stroking the child, soothing it. It might have been selfish, perhaps, but it had been such a comfort when Liz also found herself expecting. Together they could have faced the world. And Liz was so much braver, so sure things would work out. Rachel is more fearful. The stones in the churchyard tell their own tragic tale of young mothers and days-old babies. She imagines herself lying beneath the cold clay earth. Tears well up and tremble on her lids before falling in streams of sorrow and fear. Unaware she is speaking her thoughts aloud, she whispers, 'Poor, dear Liz. Poor innocent bairn. Who could have been so cruel?'*

\*     \*     \*

In December 1832 Rachel Brook and Elizabeth Rayner, both of them single young women, were at about the same stage of pregnancy. We know from Rachel's testimony that Elizabeth was 'fifteen or sixteen weeks gone' and was no longer wearing her pocket, a type of purse made of fabric and tied around the waist. It may be that Elizabeth had stopped wearing her pocket because it called attention to her changing shape. The fact she was not wearing it on the night she died probably rules out an *ad hoc* robbery that went wrong. Although there were many vagrants on the highways of England at this time, there are a number of reasons why an attack by a stranger is unlikely. Firstly, on a holiday evening in a close-knit community a stranger would have been noticed very quickly. Secondly, surely a man intent on getting money would have chosen a more likely victim. Thirdly, a random killing is rare: the vast majority of murderers are known to their victims.

To return, then, to the pregnancies – doubtless these would have occasioned a torrent of gossip, but how condemning would the local reaction have been, and what would the pregnancies have meant for the alleged fathers?

Throughout history, illegitimacy has evoked disapproval, yet at the start of the nineteenth century it was not heavily stigmatised. At a time without any but the most haphazard and basic contraception, it was accepted that unplanned, unwanted pregnancies happened sometimes, and so a *laissez-faire* attitude prevailed. Having a child out of wedlock did not necessarily prevent a girl marrying at a later date, either the father of her child or, indeed, a different man. If her family were willing and able to support her, or the man in question accepted his responsibilities, the situation was not considered a problem.

However, pregnancy outside marriage took on a wholly different aspect when the young woman was from the lowest class. Then the result could be destitution, not just for her but for her parents and siblings too. The poorest in society lived on the very edge of survival and a girl's wages were sometimes the only thing that prevented a family from slipping over the line of subsistence into total penury. When this happened the parish was obliged to step in.

In order to keep beggars and their ilk alive, poor laws had been enacted over the centuries, making every parish responsible for their own poor. Money was raised through the poor rate, a tax levied on the wealthiest members of the community. This rate was set and administered by the overseers of the poor, men of high standing in the community who were elected by the churchwardens and magistrate. Consequently, the more poor people there were in a parish the higher the poor rate. Throughout the country between 1750 and 1820 this had doubled as real per capita expenditure. By the 1830s people who paid the poor rate were becoming increasingly resentful about it.

The minutes for the Hartshead vestry meeting on 6 August read: 'The overseer of the poor, namely Joshua Fitton, made application for a rate for the relief of the poor when the following rate was granted of two shillings in the pound.' Whether it was granted grudgingly or not is unrecorded.

In order to keep the poor rate as low as possible, it was necessary to avoid having single mothers in the parish. Where possible she was returned to her parish of birth, but if she had right of residency the only option was to try and discover the name of the father by questioning her. Once the putative father was named, an order for maintenance and the cost of delivering the child would be issued by the churchwardens and overseers of the poor. The parish constable would ensure that these orders (known as bastardy bonds) were implemented. If the father defaulted on them, the mother could have him arrested on a warrant from the magistrate, and imprisoned until he agreed to fulfil his responsibilities; his possessions could be sold towards covering the debt. The cost incurred was not small: it could be paid as a lump sum to the parish of £40 minimum or fixed at a weekly rate of around 2s for a labourer and 3s 6d for a master craftsman or farmer.

So what kind of impact would this have made on the living of Thomas Ramsden or his apprentices? If, for example, John Brearley was the father of Elizabeth's child and she named him as such, how much did he have to lose? Would he have had to relinquish his apprenticeship, and would that have blighted his future earning power? How far was his future under serious threat?

An apprenticeship was usually set up between the apprentice's parents or guardians and a master craftsman, who was usually a relative or friend. A legal agreement (indenture) was then drawn up which stipulated the conditions of the apprenticeship, including how much the master would be paid for training the lad. Normally an apprenticeship began at the age of fourteen. The apprentice would not only work for his master but would live with him as part of his family, being clothed and fed but not paid a wage. At the age of twenty-one he would officially be allowed to carry out the trade as a journeyman.

Before 1814 becoming a father would have been disastrous for an apprentice because the apprenticeship statutes made it unlawful for a man to practise a trade until he had served a seven-year apprenticeship in it. Despite the fact that many crafts needed nothing like this length of training, the law had to be observed. Becoming a father would, therefore, have been a serious misfortune, as the young man could not trade without completing his time but would have had no income if he continued as apprentice – putting him between a rock and a hard place.

The new law of 1814 swept away this seven year condition, and a man could set himself up in any trade he wished without fear of prosecution: provided he could find customers he could work. So although an apprentice would have had to part company with his master to seek a wage, he would have been able to use the skills he had acquired to make a living. This, therefore, makes Brearley's position less fraught than it might have been several years earlier, and gives him a weaker motive for committing such a desperate act as murder.

Of course, the motive was not necessarily financial. Emotions such as jealousy and bitterness have often inspired vicious acts of revenge. As noted previously, although he had told his fellow apprentices and Rachel Brook that the child was his, there is a strong element of resentment and denial in the phrases Brearley uses, saying he had not got it all himself, and that somebody joined him at the child.

Could Brearley, then, have been driven to murder through anger at Elizabeth's unfaithfulness? Possibly. But although he states 'we were sweethearts'– a term Rachel Brook also uses to describe his relationship with Elizabeth – there is little real evidence of a close or passionate attachment. The way in which the murder was committed also lacks the obvious signs of a crime of passion. Dispatching a person by cutting their throat is an act of assassination – a cold act, committed with ruthless efficiency. A crime of passion, on the other hand, is likely to be committed in the heat of the moment and would leave numerous tell-tale cuts and bruises. If this had been the case, Elizabeth's body would surely have sustained a large number of injuries. It had not.

That John Brearley never considered Elizabeth a serious marriage prospect is supported by the fact he never visited her at her home, even though they had kept company for two or three years. The pregnancy, with its resulting pressure on him to do the right thing, must have made him very angry – but he was not a rat in a trap. If he was determined not to marry her, a far simpler solution than murder was open to him: he could simply leave the area and set up as a currier elsewhere. After all, there was no law to stop him.

While we cannot discount the above as motives, cold-blooded murder was not the only solution to Brearley's problems. We should remember, too, another powerful deterrent in existence at this time: the death penalty. Aged eighteen, would he have had the nerve to plan and carry out his 'sweetheart's' murder, knowing the hangman's noose awaited him if were caught?

Finally, being nothing more than an apprentice lad, how would he have had the authority and muscle to outface the suspicions of the villagers? Surely that requires someone considerably older, someone with power and influence. Someone like Thomas Ramsden?

# CHAPTER 14

# It is difficult suddenly to put aside a long-standing love: it is difficult, but somehow you must do it

*6 January 1833*

*Rachel jumps as a hand closes fiercely on her shoulder. Before she even turns she knows. It is Thomas Ramsden.*

*He stares at her intently, his features angular, hawk-like. 'I thought I'd find you here,' he says, speaking slowly. His hand slides from her shoulder to her stomach and rests there heavily: 'Just wanted a word. If you know what's good for you it's none o' mine. Don't forget.' He turns and sets off down the path.*

*'Tom . . . ?' she calls after him. Immediately she regrets speaking.*

*He marches back and snarls, 'Master to you! Get it? Don't you ever call me Tom again.'*

*At that moment all her fear erupts into ungovernable anger. 'I don't work for you any more – or that cow you call wife.'*

*Ramsden does not hesitate. He pushes her roughly against the tree and slams his hand across her mouth. 'See them stones? If you've a mind to lie beneath one, you're going the right way about it, because that's what happens to blabbermouths.'*

*Rachel stares at him in disbelief. Did she hear him right? He's as good as admitted it.*

*He notes the look on her face and feels satisfied he has said and done enough to scare her into silence. Part of him is sorry: he has a fondness for the lass, but needs must. Without another word he walks off. Rachel half runs, half staggers to the church porch.*

*       *       *

As a master currier, Thomas Ramsden's income was around 30*s* a week. With this earning capacity he was part of the aristocracy of master craftsmen. He would also have had income from the farms he worked, so he was by no means poor. The maintenance to be paid out for an illegitimate child would, nevertheless, have made a significant dent in his income, particularly bearing in mind that he had three apprentices, a wife, five children (with another on the way) and possibly a brother or two to support. To be accused of fathering his maid-servant's child would be bad financially, but there was also his reputation and standing in the village to consider.

We have already noted Ramsden's position as surveyor of the highways, and the networking opportunities and status this conferred. His business dealings in farms and land also reveal great energy and enterprise. With friends among other successful entrepreneurial families, such as the Goldthorps, Widdops, Brearleys and Listers, Thomas Ramsden was a man on the up. If a young woman had named him as father to her illegitimate child, the repercussions would have been severe for both his income and status.

But how likely is it Ramsden was responsible for Rachel's or Elizabeth's pregnancy? To retrace our steps a little, there is an intriguing comment in Rachel's statement: 'The deceased had slept with me once or twice at Thomas Ramsden's' – a point confirmed by Betty Rayner, Elizabeth's mother. Adding fuel to the fire, Rachel then relates how one evening when she and Elizabeth were returning from Oakenshaw Fair with another friend, Martha Walker, 'Thomas Ramsden came home with us.' Whether anything happened on the night of Oakenshaw Fair or not, Rachel's testimony proves, at the very least, that Thomas knew Elizabeth far better than he admits in his deposition. If, in addition, his wife's suspicions about Thomas and Rachel were correct, is it possible he was facing the disgrace of being named by not just one but two young women?

We know that Elizabeth was about four months into her pregnancy when she was murdered, which suggests she became pregnant in late August or early September. We know, too, from George Pratt's deposition that Rachel Brook was pregnant during the coroner's court enquiry, and that Ramsden's wife, Ann, was jealous of her.

The outcome of Rachel's pregnancy is recorded in the parish records: on 28 April 1833, four months after Elizabeth's murder, Rachel's daughter, Matilda Brook, was baptised. The entry space for father is ominously blank: she names neither Thomas Ramsden nor George Pratt as father. This baptism date, while useful, only allows us to estimate when Rachel became pregnant, as we do not have a record of how old Matilda was when she was baptised. We can, however, estimate the onset of Rachel's pregnancy within certain parameters. The most likely possibility is that she became pregnant at the end of July or the beginning of August, and the baptism was conducted soon after Matilda's birth. Any earlier, and Rachel would be leaving it rather late in the pregnancy to persuade George Pratt to marry her. This means she conceived only a matter of three or four weeks before Elizabeth. If Oakenshaw Fair took place in August, Thomas returning from there with the girls takes on additional significance, as it certainly implies Rachel, Elizabeth and Thomas were socialising together. Had they both developed an attachment to him? And if so, why? Why would two single girls involve themselves with the same married man?

Perhaps we need to view Thomas Ramsden from a young woman's viewpoint. As far as Rachel and Elizabeth were concerned, here was a wealthy, high status man in his prime, probably possessed of charm and charisma, who must have made their own 'sweethearts' pale by comparison. Being young women of a free and easy lifestyle, they may have enjoyed and encouraged his attentions. The heady mixture of youthful flirtation and holiday mood on the evening of Oakenshaw Fair could have sown the seeds of a love triangle.

From Ramsden's viewpoint, here were two young women enjoying his flirtation with them. Perhaps he believed he could enjoy their favours without much fear of the consequences: after all, they were, or had been, his apprentices' girlfriends, and he held considerable power over both the girls and his apprentices. But what if he was wrong about his powers of persuasion? What if, instead of complying meekly with his demands, the girls decided to make Thomas shoulder the responsibility of their pregnancies?

If, in addition, we consider what we know about the way in which Elizabeth and Rachel revealed the names of the putative fathers, then in both cases there is something not quite right. Elizabeth seems to have been peculiarly coy about naming Brearley. Indeed, it seems the only people she told were Brearley himself and

Rachel. Why such secrecy? Was she playing a game of dare with Ramsden, threatening to name him if he did not support her, while holding Brearley in reserve if Ramsden called her bluff?

In Rachel's case, there is the whole question of whether she and George were even in a relationship at the time she became pregnant. In his deposition George Pratt neither accepts nor denies responsibility for her pregnancy, but does maintain it is over a year since they were together. If this is true, it is surprising Rachel should have tried to make him take responsibility, and raises the question of whether she was put under pressure to do so by Ramsden.

One thing is sure. As master, Thomas Ramsden was in a position to exert pressure on George and John – perhaps by a combination of threat and bribery – to marry away his problems. This would certainly have been a neat solution, but could only work if all involved agreed. If they refused, the outlook for him was bleak. One illegitimate child would be bad enough, but to be named as father of two would have occasioned outrage and a severe financial penalty through bastardy bonds. In effect, a fifth of his income for the next fourteen years would disappear. This would have hurt him hard at a time when he was starting to make his mark. All things considered, he had a lot to lose if either young woman named him. And if both named him . . . well, that would have been catastrophic.

CHAPTER 15

# The man's desire is for the woman: the woman's desire is rarely other than for the desire of the man

*Sir George sits at the window of the oak room, staring out towards the fish pond where a heron has just landed in an ungainly flurry. He can hardly believe that it is almost a month since the murder of Elizabeth Rayner. It is frustrating and perplexing. The village has raised £100 for the reward, and £100 is a mighty sum. Why, even to master craftsmen it is a third of a year's income, and to labourers it is wealth beyond the dreams of avarice. And yet nothing. He thought he knew these people, but now he is starting to suspect he does not know the first thing about them. He is also deeply disappointed that the second inquiry, held a week ago on 24 January at the Armytage Arms, has produced no new leads. If he is honest, he must admit it was a complete shambles.*

*A polite cough alerts Sir George to the presence of his footman, Haley, who announces the arrival of the Reverend Thomas Atkinson.*

*'Good morning, Sir George,' the vicar begins deferentially, but Sir George is already ushering him into the library.*

*'I spent all yesterday evening reviewing the evidence, Vicar. A couple of matters on which I'd like your thoughts.'*

*'Of course,' replies Atkinson, well aware that the expression of his thoughts will probably be limited to yes and no. Still, there are worse things to do on a sharp January morning than sit sipping a glass of fine claret in the comfort of Kirklees Hall. He arranges his features into an expression of rapt attention and prepares to nod judiciously at the proper junctures.*

*'First, forget the poppycock of the second inquiry. Those witnesses had too much time to concoct new alibis. We must concentrate our efforts on*

75

the depositions before the coroner. Now, you recall my original theory?'

Atkinson nods and rapidly gathers his thoughts. He seems to remember a number of theories, but assumes Sir George is referring to the first, the one that concerns the currier, Ramsden.

'Well,' continues Sir George, 'it is the one to which I keep returning, hence it is the strongest. But I should like to dispense with a couple of points before binding myself to it entirely. Elizabeth's brother Robert – what do you make of him?' Before the vicar can offer an opinion, Sir George is off again. 'I know he sounds about as bright as a bucket of pigswill, but does that hide a native cunning?'

'Perhaps . . .' The vicar makes a second attempt to offer his view, but is cut off.

'You see, he causes her to go home for a false reason. Why? A joke, he says. But not a very witty joke, eh? One that leads to her death. Could he have had a more malevolent motive?'

The vicar says nothing. He is expecting Sir George to resume his discourse and is quite shocked when Sir George prompts, 'Well? What do you say?'

'I've heard of families so ashamed of a daughter's behaviour that they've caused her great harm – but not unto death,' says the vicar. 'Besides, she was by all accounts well liked in the village, if a little wild, and her father in particular was most fond of her. And, of course, she was not the first in her family to find herself with child outside holy matrimony.'

'Quite right. Yet the perpetrator of a murder is often found within the victim's family, so we cannot ignore that. Added to which, these villagers live so cheek by jowl that all kinds of unnatural communications can occur.'

'I think that's most unlikely,' exclaims Atkinson with some force. 'William Rayner is head of that family and a God-fearing, church-going man. He wouldn't allow anything so improper, I'm sure of it.' He pauses to settle his indignation and a new thought occurs to him. 'Of course, there is the matter of Robert's shoes. He made quite a song and dance about the ones he wore in court being the same as those he wore on the night of the murder. But why mention them? If there had been blood on them he could easily have washed them clean, and thus they prove nothing.'

Sir George flaps his handkerchief dismissively. 'That's where you're mistaken. I once got blood on my top boots during a hunt – they never came quite clean again no matter how Wilkinson scrubbed them. So I've no quarrel with his shoes. No, no. To be frank, I don't seriously consider him a suspect. Nevertheless I can't help but wonder if the joke was his idea. Could someone else have put him up to winkling her out of Widow Glover's?'

*'But if that's the case, why not report it to us? Surely he would wish his sister's attacker to be punished. And the reward money he could claim —that would make a great difference to a family such as the Rayners.'*

*Sir George's fist makes heavy contact with the table, causing Atkinson to flinch. 'Exactly! That's what puzzles me. A hundred pounds going begging, and not a sniff at it from a single witness. Why?'*

*'Because,' begins the vicar, quite pleased at the novelty of a two-way conversation with the baronet. The novelty does not last.*

*'Because,' cuts in Sir George, 'they are all afraid! Someone is threatening them. There's only one thing more we can do. I shall write to the Home Secretary this very day to request an increase to the reward money. Lord Melbourne is a benevolent man, and I'm sure I can prevail on him to grant it.'*

*The Reverend Mr Atkinson nods sagely, but is not optimistic.*

\*     \*     \*

Of all the depositions, Robert Rayner's is the only one where the clerk records some of his words in Yorkshire dialect. We read in his deposition that he told Elizabeth, 'I think it will be as well for thee to be at home. Go and see if my mother does not want thee to do something this evening.'

At the time all the witnesses would have spoken with a strong Yorkshire accent, but 'you' is only transcribed as 'thee' in Robert's deposition. This may have been an error on the clerk's part, or he may have left it in deliberately to indicate Robert's rougher social standing. Taken together with Robert's joking 'nonsense', it conjures up a humorous, rough and ready character, given to playing the fool. His extrovert nature may also have made him popular with the opposite sex, as we learn that five young women from the Alms Houses accompanied him to Brighouse.

The big question regarding Robert is whether the joke he played on Elizabeth was an innocent jest or whether he was duped into giving her the false message. If the latter, it is astonishing he did not report it to anyone. We have noted the signs of sibling affection between Robert and Liz, so surely he would wish to have her death avenged. But what if he was unable to speak up? What if someone had something on him?

Even today, with the benefit of modern policing and witness protection schemes, there are many cases where people are simply too frightened to come forward. How much more difficult must it have been in the 1830s? Hartshead and Clifton had no regular police force. Law and order was administered by one constable and one magistrate. Streets were dark and often lonely. There was no forensic science. No detective constables. Threats from a hard man with willing accomplices and useful connections were not to be taken lightly. Add to this the burden of proof that the crown prosecution needed to establish, and silence does not seem such a bad option.

*    *    *

*Robert has not been the same since his sister's murder. The weight has rolled off him, leaving his once thickly muscled arms thin and sinewy. He blames himself a hundred times a day. His mother has tried to comfort him, saying he couldn't have known what the outcome of the joke would be, but she doesn't know the whole story. The truth is there was more to it than brotherly nonsense.*

*Looking back, he could tell at the time there was something amiss; he could feel it in his bones. For a start, he should have been suspicious John Brearley sent George Pratt to ask the favour: 'Brearley wants a word with your Liz but she's not talking to him. Could you get her out of Hannah Glover's for him? Don't say why, though.' At first he'd refused. But then Pratt had said, 'Brearley says he'll talk Ramsden into getting his deer hides elsewhere if you don't. Knowing him, he means it.'*

*That was the last thing Robert needed. For the past year he and a gang of lads – including Joseph Stott and George's brothers, Joseph and Charles – had been making a pretty penny poaching deer on the Kirklees estate. With Thomas Ramsden willing to buy the hides, no questions asked, Robert had got used to the little luxuries the extra income afforded. The threat of losing it was a potent one – too potent.*

*So now, as much as Robert has tried to persuade himself that obliging Brearley was nothing to do with Liz's murder, a sick, aching hollow in his chest contradicts him. But should he give voice to what he knows? Could he bear his father's disappointment and anger? Robert thinks not.*

# CHAPTER 16

# Let me tell you about the very rich.
# They are different to you and me

With the investigation into the murder stalled, Sir George Armytage sent a letter to the Home Secretary, Lord Melbourne, on 31 January 1833. The letter begs to inform his lordship that a 'cruel murder was committed on the 31st December last or on the 1st of January in a wood called Clifton Wood in the township of Clifton in the West Riding of the county of York and belonging to me, within a short distance of my mansion house at Kirklees.'

The two references to his property imply that Sir George's outrage at the crime was matched equally by the fact it was committed on his land, which presents him in a rather egotistical, unflattering light. However, he needed to be as persuasive as possible, and by referring to his mansion and land he was reminding Lord Melbourne that they were members of the same club – the aristocracy – and consequently under an obligation to grant each other favours.

Sir George continues the letter by informing Melbourne he has enclosed the depositions before the coroner for 'your Lordship's inspection', and that the jury had reached a verdict of 'wilful murder by person or persons unknown'. Next he professes that investigations have been made by himself and the inhabitants of Clifton, but admits: 'I am sorry to say that we cannot as yet find any clue to lead to the discovery of the murderer.'

Finally he gets to the crux of the matter: the appeal for money. Having explained that a £100 reward has been raised by himself and the people of Clifton, Sir George makes his request in the most circuitous way imaginable: 'If your Lordship thinks that an additional reward from His Majesty may lead to a discovery of this most cruel murder, the inhabitants of Clifton and myself will most gratefully acknowledge His Majesty's condescension in complying with our request for whatever sum he may think it proper to grant.' (Phew!)

The ingratiating tone worked. After briefly describing the murder, the *London Gazette* of 8 February 1833 reported: 'His Majesty, for the better apprehending and bringing to justice the persons concerned in the murder before mentioned, is hereby pleased to promise His most gracious pardon to any one of them (except the person who actually committed the same) who shall discover his accomplice or accomplices therein, so that he, she, or they may be apprehended and convicted thereof.' The report concludes with the information that more money has been granted towards the reward: 'And as a further encouragement, a reward of ONE HUNDRED POUNDS is hereby offered by the Right Honourable the Lords Commissioners of His Majesty's Treasury.'

Sir George's plea had proved successful. The reward now stood at £200, and locally this was reported in the *Halifax Guardian and Huddersfield and Bradford Advertiser* on 23 February. If he believed this was the key that would unlock the case, however, he was sadly mistaken.

*   *   *

*George Pratt clumps into the currying workshop to discover Thomas Ramsden flanked by John Brearley and Joseph Stott. Thomas is holding a copy of the local newspaper and they are all engrossed in reading it.*

*'What's up?' George asks.*

*'Nowt for you to bother about,' answers Brearley, off hand with Pratt as usual.*

*Ignoring the comment, George joins them, and quickly focuses on the item of interest. 'Two hundred pounds! Bloody hell! That's a lot of brass. How come it's gone up so much?'*

*'Armytage,' answers Ramsden. 'He'll have written to the bigwigs in London for it.'*

*George cannot help but take a certain pleasure in the worried expressions of Brearley and Stott. For the first time in his life he is glad to be on the edges, glad to be excluded. Inside he is grinning fit to burst, but disguises it well and says with apparent innocence, 'Well, let's hope this is enough to bring out the truth. Let's hope Liz's murderer is brought to justice, eh?'*

*Ramsden looks up from the page and stares straight into George's eyes as if to see inside his head and read his thoughts. 'Aye,' he says. 'Let's hope the bastard swings for it.'*

*George feels his face turn hot as blood surges to his cheeks. He has not yet told anyone about John Brearley asking Robert Rayner to get Liz from the Alms Houses. Neither has he mentioned the scrap of material he found in the grate on New Year's Day – only about an inch square, but with a tell-tale brown stain of blood. Of course it had meant nothing to him then, because he didn't know Liz Rayner was lying dead in Clifton Wood. He'd left the scrap where it was and lit the fire. Now, though, he wishes he had it still. He'd bet a pound to a penny he knows whose shirt it came from.*

*Later on New Year's Day, after he'd seen Liz's body all crumpled and blood-splattered, he'd been close to telling the constable what he knew. But he hadn't. He is vulnerable – or at least his brothers are – a fact Ramsden and Brearley are very well aware of. Even so, murder is a damned sight worse than a bit of snecking, isn't it? Surely the magistrate would see that. Except the magistrate is Sir George and the snecking was on his land. What to do, then? Two hundred pounds. He could leave Clifton, set up somewhere new. Maybe he should go to see the constable this very day . . .*

*Ramsden flings the paper on the workbench and gives George a friendly smile. 'Now then, George,' he says. 'Happen it's time for you to take a bit more responsibility. How about you come wi' me to choose some hides, eh?'*

*George glances at Brearley. It's usually him that goes off to places with Ramsden. Brearley looks a bit put out. Good. Let him be the one left doing the dog's work for a change. Ramsden puts a fatherly arm around George's shoulders and they go into the yard.*

*As the cart rumbles along Sheep Cote Lane past the wood, George finds his gaze pulled towards its dark interior. He has always hated it. Unable to stop himself, he shudders.*

*'How's the family getting along?' asks Ramsden. The question is asked in cordial enough fashion, so George wonders why he feels nervous about giving his answer.*

*'Well enough,' he replies.*

*'Brearley said he had a right good evening with your brothers on New Year's Eve. Reckons they supped their weight in ale, though.'*

George is certain now that this chat has a darker agenda than Ramsden's carefree tone suggests. He sinks into a wary silence.

'How old's your youngest brother?' asks Ramsden. Without waiting for reply he continues, 'Lads can be a bit wild at sixteen. I heard tell of one youth, even younger than that, got transported. Well, he would have, only when the boat reached Van Diemen's Land the natives chopped him to bits. I wouldn't want a lad to end up like that.'

'Me neither,' mutters George.

'Good,' says Ramsden. 'Then you know what to do.'

# CHAPTER 17

# Because I could not stop for Death, he kindly stopped for me

*July 1836*

*It is seven o'clock on a fine spring evening. Soon the men from the village will start arriving at the Black Horse to sup longed-for pints of ale to slake their thirsts after the hard labour of the fields, pits and workshops.*

*James Pease leans against the counter. He is in melancholy mood but doesn't know why. In his imagination he peoples the little room with the men who drank there twenty years or more ago. It was there, by the fireplace, the infamous Luddite George Mellor stood to address them. A tall young man with curly flaxen hair and bright, passionate eyes – a rabble-rouser and a half he was. That night he'd recruited over thirty Clifton and Hartshead men to join the attack on Rawfold's Mill. The plan was to destroy the hated cropping machines that threatened the handcroppers' livelihoods. Pease could remember the heat of emotion even now. But what bloody fools they'd been. As if their puny weapons could ever have hoped to triumph over the soldiers in the battle that followed. Two of Mellor's comrades had paid for their rashness with mortal gunshot wounds. And Mellor, in an act of bloody revenge, had later murdered the mill owner, Horsfall. He'd swung for it an' all. Could it really be more than twenty years ago?*

*Suddenly his reverie is broken. Thomas Ramsden appears at the counter and chucks a couple of pennies down. 'Pint of ale, Jim,' he says.*

*The innkeeper pours a pint but says nothing. He is in no hurry to chat with Ramsden. The village's attitude of icy neutrality may not have frozen Ramsden out, but it must make his life uncomfortable. Surely.*

'I hear Sir George is badly,' says Ramsden as he picks up the glass. He is careful to wear a bland expression, but Pease notices a nerve jump at the corner of his mouth.

'Like you'd care,' says Pease.

Ramsden shrugs. 'I've nowt against the old lad.'

'He's on his last legs, so they say. Not likely to see out the summer. Still, it comes to all of us in the end,' he adds, his lugubrious features well suited to the pronouncement. Then, before Ramsden can engage him in any further talk, Pease turns away and picks up a clay pipe which he proceeds to fill with studious care. Once the thick tobacco leaves are tamped down to his satisfaction, he lights up and inhales deeply, which at once produces a scale of choking coughs that inflame his face.

Despite the ferocity of the coughing, over in the corner Ramsden keeps his eyes firmly fixed on his newspaper, while the kitchen maid comes running in from the back room and hands Pease a glass of water. Somehow he splutters it down. For a few moments he breathes heavily, leaning against the counter for support. This bloody nuisance has been plaguing him since Christmas. He just can't seem to shake it off.

'You all right, Master?' asks the maid, her little face scrunched up in anxiety. He nods, but sits down behind the bar, sipping the rest of the water carefully. Every so often he glances thoughtfully in Ramsden's direction. If Ramsden's bothered about the gossip surrounding him since the coroner's inquiry, he makes a damn good job of hiding it. Most men would have put as many miles between them and the murder scene as possible, maybe setting sail for America to start again in a young country. That's what most folks expected Ramsden to do, but here he sits like a spider in his web. Pease thinks he knows why. It's about your territory, and Ramsden'll not be hounded out by a few wagging tongues. Even so, Pease wonders how he holds it all together. Doesn't it put a terrible strain on a man when he knows what everybody's thinking about him?

The innkeeper is suddenly aware of his chest again – it's like hoops being tightened round a barrel. When is this bloody cough going to clear up?

*　　*　　*

Sir George Armytage died on 14 July 1836, all his investigations into the murder coming to naught. James Pease, innkeeper of the Black Horse, followed him to Hartshead churchyard a little over a month later, being buried there on 19 August at the age of fifty-six.

As for Thomas Ramsden, he remained where he was and thrived. At least – for a while.

*   *   *

By the 1950s the murder had become the shadow of a memory, only referred to in the locality as a way to dissuade children from playing in the wood. Margaret Sharp, former resident of Clifton and local historian, recalls: 'When we were children we were warned not to enter that part of the wood because there had been a murder there. That it had happened more than a hundred years previously was never mentioned.'

In 1833 those involved in trying to solve the crime – Sir George Armytage, Constable Charles Ramsden, the coroner Michael Stocks Junior and their colleagues – were hampered by primitive investigative methods and a wall of silence from the community. When the tempting £200 reward failed to produce an informant, the investigation faltered, then came to a final halt.

Although today we are unable to interview witnesses or examine the crime scene, we do have an angle the contemporary investigators did not possess – that is, the ability to trace Elizabeth's family and friends in the succeeding years, with the help of parish and census records. These give us a good idea about whose fortunes declined, who prospered and who was most affected by the murder. Do any of their circumstances provide fresh clues?

In 1841, just eight years after the inquest into the death of Elizabeth Rayner, the first of the modern censuses made its entrance. Earlier ones had done no more than record bare numerical data; this one was much more ambitious as it included relationships of household members, their occupations and their ages – rounded down to the nearest five for adults. If we turn to the entry for the Ramsdens, it is immediately apparent things have changed.

We find the household made up of Thomas, his wife and their five children – George (seventeen), Mary (thirteen), John (eleven), Sarah (nine) and Charles (seven), along with Thomas's sister Mary (thirty-eight). Surprisingly there are no apprentices living with them. By the next census, ten years later, Thomas is also absent.

A table tomb in Hartshead churchyard explains why: 'Thomas Ramsden, currier, died April 20th 1847.' How he died we do not know – an infectious illness, a cut turned to blood poisoning, the possibilities are endless and uncertain – but the grave supplies us with other tantalising insights. The most remarkable thing about it, apart from its substantial presence, is the inclusion of Thomas's occupation: currier. This single word says a great deal about his feelings towards his business. It is as a currier he wants to be remembered. But why? Exactly what had he achieved that made him so proud of his occupation?

A clue to the answer can be found in the following censuses. In 1851 his widow, Ann, aged forty-eight, is head of the household, her occupation farmer and currier. She has taken over the reins of the business, no doubt enlisting sons George, John and Charles to help her. But not only has she kept the family's business concerns going, by 1861 we find her sufficiently successful to be recorded as a 'currier and farmer of 48 acres, employing three men and two currier's assistants'. In 1859 she had also taken on the tenancy of the Armytage Arms public house, adding yet another string to her bow. The 1861 census finds only the second son, John, at home (at thirty-one a tragically young widower), with granddaughter Lydia Ann (ten), an apprentice, Joseph Robinson (twenty) and a servant, Sarah Ann Morrison (sixteen).

Ann doubtless learnt a great deal about currying from her husband, but it is abundantly clear she was possessed of a sharp business brain. In the newspaper obituary for her son Charles in August 1893, a passage recalls his mother: 'She was a shrewd businesswoman and many of the older generation of traders in the Spen Valley retain lively recollections of her business capabilities during the years which followed her husband's death.' Of course, by the time Thomas died she had the advantage of her eldest son, George, being a fully trained master currier, and John being part way through his apprenticeship. But even so, her success would have required a strong base on which to build: Thomas, it seems, had seen to that.

Thomas's will, made the day before he died, is short, to the point and unfortunately does not itemise his bequests or give a valuation of his estate. Having bequeathed all his possessions to 'my dear wife', the final sentence requests that she 'bring up those of my dear children, which are not yet brought up, in a decent and respectable way as her circumstances will admit of and that she keep home for them as long as they keep single and behave themselves with propriety'. The puzzling question here is, does this desire for his children to behave with propriety come from a man of blameless past, or is it the remorse of a guilty conscience speaking?

By the time Ann signed her own will on Thursday 18 February 1869, the property and money to be shared out was significant: after debts and funeral expenses have been accounted for, John inherited £300, George £150, Mary £200, Sarah £150 and Lydia Ann £100. The tenancies of two farms, Low and Upper Farm were bequeathed to John and Charles, respectively, providing the landlord, Sir George Armytage (the 5th baronet, grandson of the previous Sir George) 'shall admit them as tenants and upon further trust to pay the residue of the money to arise from the conversion of my personal estate into money and the amount to arise from the valuation of tenant right to my sons John and Charles share and share alike'. Curiously, Ann divides up the bequests from her farming interests between her son John and a farmer called John Brown. Brown's relationship to Ann is unclear, but a glance at his background seems to rule out kinship. He was not local, his place of birth being Sicklinghall, North Yorkshire, and he had not married into the Ramsden family, his wife Mary Ann being from Hampsthwaite in the same county. We find John Brown in the 1851 census described as a farmer of 12 acres and a schoolmaster (an unusual combination), but where he was teaching at this point is unclear. A year later, however, he was appointed schoolmaster of Clifton school and remained in this post for nine years. The school was in Common Side, not far from the Ramsdens' home and workshop, so perhaps it was as a neighbour Ann got to know him. As he was a well-educated man and also had farming interests, perhaps Ann discussed her business decisions with him. Whatever the case, she felt warmly enough towards him to remember him in her will.

Another point of note is that it is Ann's second son John, not the eldest, George, who benefited most from the bequests. This may be because when John was widowed he returned to live with his mother. He inherited all the household effects, 'as well as the currier's tools belonging to me (Ann), for his own use'.

The last census return for John in 1871 gives his occupation as currier and farmer of 35 acres. He has no children of his own, but was caring for his sister Sarah's daughter, Lydia Ann, and two nephews, Henry and Thomas.

George and Charles also thrived, marrying well. George married Ann Womersley and went to live with her and her widowed mother, also Ann. Widow Womersley was not without means, being a farmer of 8 acres. There seems to have been something of a power struggle, as both she and her son-in-law claimed the status of head of household. George's wife, Ann, was also an industrious young woman, giving her occupation as dressmaker, despite having a two-year-old daughter, Mary. George must have learned the value of having a strong wife from observing his mother's determination and drive.

Charles's life followed a similar pattern. He married and continued the family occupation, being recorded as a leather dresser, but by the 1871 census we find him as a farmer of 60 acres and licensed victualler of the Armytage Arms, a pub that was to remain in the family for years to come. Charles was a genial and popular figure in Clifton, as is evidenced by his obituary. This notes his death with 'sincere regret' and describes him in glowing terms. His son Jemie was later regarded locally with the same affection and high esteem.

One final, rather ironic piece of information is that in the 1851 census Thomas's daughter Sarah, at the age of just eighteen, was a single mother. How must Ann Ramsden have felt about her daughter's situation, especially given Thomas's dying wish that his children would live respectable lives? Was she transported back eighteen years to those inconsiderate pregnancies of Elizabeth Rayner and Rachel Brook? The census entry for the household tells us all we need to know – the child, Lydia Ann Ramsden, is recorded not as Sarah's daughter but as Ann's.

Everything we have discovered about Thomas Ramsden gives us the idea of a man with a powerful presence – a man of considerable pride and ambition, but also charm when required – a man who had the wherewithal to dominate weaker characters. If anyone had the means and the drive to silence potential witnesses, surely he was the one.

# CHAPTER 18

# And we forget because we must, and not because we will

For William and Betty Rayner, the death of their next-to-eldest daughter was one tragedy in many: they had lost Mary Ann and Annis during their infancy and their eldest son, Crispin, at twenty-one. But the fact Elizabeth was murdered doubtless made her loss that much harder to bear. And as if this were not bad enough, they also had the constant hurt of seeing the men they suspected of the crime, Ramsden and Brearley, going about their business in the village each day, free as birds.

For most parents the only option would have been to pack up and leave, but William and Betty were as tough as the Yorkshire grit beneath their feet, and in the 1841 census we find the family still living at Well Lane, next door but two to their old neighbour, Abigail Oldfield.

There are many motives that might have persuaded them to stay in Clifton. Perhaps they clung to the hope some evidence might yet be found to put flesh on William's accusations against Ramsden and Brearley. Being in the vicinity meant they were more likely to hear if this occurred. They may have also felt that their presence in the village might prick someone's guilty conscience and lead to a confession. Whatever their reasons, there is something dogged and stubborn in their refusal to flee – a defiant stand-off that at the very least must have made the killers uncomfortable.

\*     \*     \*

*Well Lane, 1841*

*Betty Rayner has done her best but to no avail. Her daughter Sarah sits by the fireside rocking backwards and forwards, staring fiercely at a single strawberry blonde ringlet in her lap. Betty feels she is looking at an image of herself back in 1830, and the memory turns her sick for a moment. But she wipes her eyes, catches up the broom and starts sweeping the floor. Keeping busy is the only palliative to grief she knows. But Sarah won't listen to her advice and sinks deeper into sorrow each day.*

*There comes a knock at the door. It's the census chap come to write his records about the village. Betty ushers him to the rickety old table that dominates the room. He appears younger than he probably is and has a girlish mouth upturned in a polite smile, so when he catches sight of Sarah he averts his eyes quickly and concentrates on what Betty is saying.*

*'You must excuse our Sarah, for she's had a sad loss. If you'd come to us nobbut a week since there'd have been her little lad to count as well.'*

*'I'm sorry for your trouble,' the census man says, tipping his head respectfully to Sarah.*

*'Crispin. Only two years old. He was named for his uncle. We've lost two Crispins now. Happen it's an unlucky name . . .' Betty breaks off, defeated by the effort at normality.*

*'I'm sorry,' he repeats. 'I'd leave you be, only I'm not allowed. It's the law.'*

*Mechanically, Betty gives the family's names and occupations: William, head of household, wire drawer; Robert, labourer; Simeon, labourer; John, labourer; Edmund, scholar; Joseph, grandson, scholar.*

*   *   *

At the time of the coroner's inquiry in 1833, Elizabeth's brother Robert was described as a wire drawer, and we know from his deposition that he was popular with the young women of the village – after all, five of them accompanied him to Brighouse. But his circumstances under ten years later were less buoyant. Although thirty-one years old, he was still unmarried and living at home. He had lost the security and pay of wire drawing, and instead had the much lowlier occupation of labourer. Given that records for the period continue to show large numbers of Clifton men gainfully employed in wire drawing, it is unlikely his departure from the trade was voluntary.

So what caused Robert's tumble down the social ladder? We cannot know for sure, but a possibility must be a decline in his emotional or mental health. It may be that he could not come to terms with his sister's violent death for, whether innocently meant or not, it was his 'joke' that sent Elizabeth into the arms of her attacker. Perhaps he knew more than he admitted about the murder and was tormented by a guilty conscience. Whatever the cause of his downward spiral, Robert died in April 1847, aged just thirty-seven.

The two brothers who had discovered Elizabeth's body in Clifton Wood fared rather better. By 1851 both Simeon and John had married and established their own homes: Simeon near his parents in Well Lane with wife Jane and infants Robert and Frances Ann; and John with his wife Betty in Grave Lane (now Grange Lane) with infants Elizabeth and Crispin.

As for Sarah, the eldest of the Rayners' offspring, she continued along her own unconventional path. By 1851 she had yet another illegitimate child, a one-year-old daughter called Rhoda. As with her previous children, no father's name is given in the baptismal records. But Sarah was at least now in employment, working as a card setter. Card setting involved placing wire staples into pricked leather cards, which were then used to untangle knots in wool before spinning it. The pay for this monotonous work was criminally poor – ½d for 600 staples. Did Sarah prize her independence, or resent the way she had been deserted and left to fend for herself? Was she infuriated by the inequalities that plagued women, both in their social lives and in their work? For example, her son Joseph also worked in carding, but his job of sewing leather straps onto the cards was a much less onerous task and better paid, too.

William and Betty Rayner lived on into their late seventies, and their burials are recorded in the parish register: Betty in October 1858, William in December 1861. Surprisingly, the longest lived of their offspring was the eldest, the troublesome Sarah, who lived to the ripe old age of eighty-two, her colourful but difficult life giving credence to the adage, 'What doesn't kill you makes you stronger.'

If nothing else, the Rayner family had the support network of a large family. Sarah, despite her peccadilloes, always found shelter in the family home, and doubtless Elizabeth would have too, had she lived. In contrast, the much smaller family unit of Rachel Brook and her mother Elizabeth did not enjoy such benefits. So how did the Brooks fare over the next few decades?

Penury is the key word in Elizabeth Brook's life. As one of the poorest of the poor, she lived in the Alms Houses and was a recipient of the Armytage's Wheat Dole charity. By 1841, however, she was no longer living at the Alms Houses. At first sight this suggests her fortunes had taken a turn for the better, but this is unlikely. We find her living with her granddaughter Matilda, the illegitimate child of Rachel, in a household of eight people, headed by a Mary Wright. What the relationship was between the Brooks and Wrights is difficult to establish as it is not recorded by the 1841 census, but in total the household was composed of five Wrights and a Betty Priestley, aged twelve, possibly an orphan relative. Given the size of the average cottage this must have been a squeeze.

There is no mention of Rachel Brook with them – or anywhere else in Clifton. So where had she gone, and why had she left Matilda behind? Had she died as the result of complications after childbirth? Had she married George Pratt?

The answer is that she had married – but not George. In 1838 Rachel married Francis Hill, a labourer. The 1841 census records them living a short distance from Clifton in the neighbouring village of Brighouse, with two young daughters: Ellen aged five and Hannah aged two. But why was Matilda not with them? Why had Rachel abandoned her youngest child? There are a number of possibilities.

As a labourer, Rachel's husband Francis was economically near the bottom of the heap, and may have simply refused to bear the burden of raising another man's child. In order to keep him, Rachel may have had to put his wishes before the needs of her child. However, to leave her with an elderly woman who was to all intents and purposes a pauper seems callous in the extreme. Could there be a more benevolent reason for Rachel's decision? Could it be that Matilda's natural father had developed a proprietary feeling about her? Was it he who exerted pressure on Rachel for Matilda to stay in Clifton?

\*     \*     \*

*January 1838*

*Joseph Stott is watching again. A cart has just pulled up outside the Wrights' cottage and he thinks he knows why. Rachel, her mother Elizabeth and daughter Matilda have been living with the Wrights for a few weeks, but it is too small a cottage for eight people. He leans back against the wall and waits to see what will happen.*

*Sure enough, the driver, Francis Hill, scrambles down from the cart, goes to the door and knocks. Out comes Rachel Brook followed by her mother. Rachel is carrying Matilda in her arms and the child is clinging to her with all her little might. As soon as Rachel tries to extricate herself, the little girl cries out sharply and clings all the harder. Within seconds all are crying: three generations weeping their misery into the early morning sunshine.*

*Joseph notes the child's ringlet curls and small straight nose – perfect copies of her mother's. The full-lipped mouth, though, and the dark, night-blue eyes are the father's through and through, features so shockingly exact that he wonders why his master doesn't take the opportunity to get the child out of Clifton with her mother. Joseph would be willing to bet that Francis Hill would take them both for only a little more brass: this sending off of Rachel seems only half a solution to Joseph, and he wonders at Ramsden's short sightedness. Still, it isn't his problem and he'll be leaving the village himself in a week or two.*

*With a little help from her mother, Rachel has finally uncurled the limpet-like fingers from her neck and Matilda at last succumbs to the inevitable, as her weeping subsides into shuddering gulps. Rachel loads a forlorn bundle of possessions on top of the few sticks of furniture in the back of the cart.*

*'Look after her, Mam. I know you will, only . . . you know. And if he lets so much as a week go by without paying what he's promised, let me know.'*

*'Don't fret. She'll be safe enough with me. Now go on. I'll bring her to you from time to time.'*

*'Come on, Rachel,' says Francis, helping her up onto the passenger seat. 'I've promised to get this cart back to John Widdop by six. Let's be off.'*

*He taps the flanks of the old grey nag, Nelson, with his whip. The horse starts out of his equine daydreams with a snort and the cart lurches forward.*

*'Be good for your grandma!' calls Rachel, forcing a desperate smile towards the child. Her gaze is so firmly fixed on the little family she is leaving behind that she does not see the watcher.*

*     *     *

By the 1851 census we find an Elizabeth Brook, aged seventy-two, living at Gorse Hill, in Bowling near Bradford, with her nephew George Walker, a wire drawing master employing men. Is this the same Elizabeth? Three facts suggest it is: her age, the place of birth

– Clifton – and the occupation, 'pauper and card setter'. Elizabeth Brook's life continued in poverty – her twilight years spent separated from her daughter and granddaughter, and dependent on the charity of the relatively well-off nephew and his wife.

The reason she did not move in with her daughter becomes clear when we find Rachel and her husband Francis in the 1851 census: they have four daughters and two sons, and, on a cheerful note, Rachel's first child, Matilda, is now living with them. We can be sure that on a farm labourers' wage the family would have been on the breadline, so it is no surprise Matilda and her half sisters Hannah (twelve) and Ann (nine) are all working as card setters.

Despite the hardships the Hills endured, both were still alive in 1881. The census records Rachel's age as sixty-five and Francis's as seventy-eight. Sadly, it also notes he is 'nearly blind'.

Their remaining years were probably difficult, but they had the comfort and support of having produced ten children, two of whom lived close by – the strangely named son Shepherd next door and John a few houses away. When contemplating her life, Rachel could at least be thankful that it had not ended as early and pointlessly as her long-dead friend Liz's had. Being thankful for what you had was a lesson well learnt.

# CHAPTER 19

# Fears and fancies thick upon
# me come

*December 1835*

*George Pratt is sitting at the top of Clifton Wood, peering into the inky tangle of its branches and thinking. It is a frosty winter's night, chilled by a full pale moon, but he does not feel the cold. He often comes here when he can't sleep, which means most nights. Part of him hopes for a glimpse of Liz's shadow weaving through the trees – the other half is terrified she'll appear. He thinks that if he continues his vigil long enough she will relent and come to him. He only wants to explain why he can't shop his master and Brearley.*

*Sometimes he wonders if it's the wood itself that's to blame. Even in daylight it's a place that thrums with malevolence, a place that has haunted his dreams since he was a child. It's like a huge living web, a predatory place that tolerates life but secretly yearns to destroy it – and often does. When he was a lad he and his brothers would spend whole days here, snaring rabbits for the pot, killing and skinning them. He was good at it – but he always felt the wood was watching him with resentment, waiting and biding its time.*

*Once, when he was about six years old, his brother Joseph and another lad from the village, had made him pretend to be a deer so they could hunt him. Then, when they'd caught him, they'd taken a rope, tied him to a tree and run off, shouting he would have to spend the night there.*

*For the first hour or so he'd been brave and told himself there was nothing to worry over. But then dusk had crept into the wood, smoothing the comforting edges of things until substance and shadow were so wrapped up in each other he could not tell where one ended and the other began. That was when the voice began whispering at him in sounds that eddied and bubbled like a stream. What was it saying?*

*And then suddenly he had seen it – not for long, but long enough: a maggot-white skull, the empty sockets lit with a point of fierce red light, the grin sharpened by vulpine teeth – peeking out at him from the branches above. His bravery utterly crushed, he screamed out his panic until he thought his lungs must explode. Which is how his father had found him, shrieking in abject terror, almost unable to breathe.*

*That his brother earned the thrashing of his life for the mean prank was of little consolation. From that moment the spirit of the wood haunted George and would not let him go.*

*Suddenly he is aware of a noise behind him, and he looks round. It is Brearley and Stott. He guesses they have been there for a while.*

*'Who you talking to?' asks Brearley, scanning their surroundings.*

*George says nothing. It may have been the wood that murdered Elizabeth Rayner but the spirit didn't strike alone; it needed its henchmen.*

*'Come on,' says Stott. 'Me and Brearley will help you home. Looks like you've had a skinful.'*

*Ignoring Brearley's proffered hand, Pratt rises unsteadily to his feet and slurs, 'I'd as soon touch the devil's.'*

*'Piss off then,' snarls Brearley, and makes off down Sheep Cote Lane.*

*'What's up wi' you?' asks Stott. 'He's only trying to help.'*

*At that moment George is overcome with the need to confide in someone. A hopeful idea pops into his head. 'I suppose they've got summat on you an' all, Joe. But that doesn't mean we have to keep us mouths shut forever. Happen we could go together and tell what we know.'*

*'What you on about?' says Joseph, eyes stretched innocently wide.*

*George attempts to tap his nose in a knowing manner but misses and taps the air. He belches. 'I bet you know as much as I do about yon devils. If it weren't for my brothers, I'd have been up to Kirklees Hall like a shot – two hundred the richer an' all.'*

*Stott shifts a little uneasily and grabs George by the waistcoat to make him move. 'You're talking daft. Come on, it's time you were in bed.'*

*George sways momentarily, trying hard to focus on Stott's face to read his eyes. A sudden wave of nausea convulses his stomach, making him vomit.*

\*   \*   \*

*January 1836*

*John Brearley and Joseph Stott are about to side away their tools for the day when the master steps into the workshop. Ramsden is a man whose moods affect those around him as effectively as weather, and it is as if a sharp arctic blast accompanies him. Despite the passing of three years, unspoken hostility from the villagers towards the master and his apprentices continues, but it has not affected the business and they have hardened themselves to the discomfort of cold stares and narrowed eyes. But this evening Brearley and Stott can tell the status quo has been disturbed – Ramsden's stiffened jaw all but yells there's a problem.*

'Sit down, lads. *There's stuff we need to talk about,' he says.*

*Brearley chucks down his knife like a schoolboy petulant at being discovered in a lie.* 'I've said I'll marry her,' *he snaps before Ramsden can say more.* 'I've been up to see John Green and it's sorted. April.'

'Woah! Don't bite my bleeding head off. This isn't about you and Sarah Ann. You'll be your own man in a couple of weeks, so it's none of my business.'

*Brearley frowns and sits down on the currying workbench.* 'What is it then?'

'It's Pratt – fighting again. He's acting like he's not right in the head. T' other day I caught him talking to himself, and I didn't like what I heard. He's dangerous.'

*A knowing glance passes between the two young men, which goes unnoticed by Ramsden.* 'I want him and his brothers out of Clifton and the sooner the better. Joseph, when you go back to Rastrick you mun take him with you.'

'I'm not living with him!' *protests Joseph.*

'I never said you had to. He can live with his brothers. But I want you nearby to keep an eye on him.'

'You should have made him marry Rachel,' *says Brearley.* 'A brat would have kept him too busy to worry over what's past.'

'You don't get it, do you? Pratt doesn't like women.' *Ramsden's full-lipped mouth twists into its mocking smile.* 'He could no more marry Rachel than I could marry you.'

*Brearley looks confused.* 'What's he fretting over then? If he doesn't like the lasses, what's he so bothered about Liz for?'

*Joseph Stott looks at his friend closely. All these years and it has never truly struck him before – Brearley really can't tell why George Pratt feels guilty about knowing what he knows.* 'Maybe he thinks God'll punish him,' *says Joseph, hurriedly.* 'But any road,' *he continues, turning to*

*Ramsden, 'what makes you think Pratt and his brothers will do as you say?'*

*'I'll put a lot of business their way if they get their sorry arses out of Clifton. They'd be fools to refuse me – which they aren't because they've already agreed. I think they know as well as I do it'd be best for George. Out of sight, out of mind, eh?'*

*'Whatever you say, Master,' says Brearley.*

\*     \*     \*

After serving their seven-year apprenticeship, John Brearley, George Pratt and Joseph Stott were armed with all the skills and experience they needed to work as curriers. There were three options open to them: each could work as a one-man operation; they could take employment at an established currying workshop; or, the most ambitious option, they could start their own workshop, employing other men and training apprentices.

Interestingly, only John Brearley remained in Clifton at this point. We know from censuses that he stayed in the village until at least 1851, but by 1863 at the latest he was working in Halifax. As for the others, Joseph Stott returned to his home village of Rastrick, about 2 miles away, an understandable move. That George Pratt also moved to Rastrick is harder to explain. In the 1841 census we find him living in an area of the village called Snake Hill, near the River Calder. With him are his brothers Joseph and Charles, who are joiners; George and Ellen Hibbert (possibly his married sister); and a land valuer, John Goldthorp, aged sixty. The latter is probably the John Goldthorp mentioned by George in his deposition as the person at whose house he spent New Year's Eve. So were there advantages for the Pratt brothers in the move to Rastrick?

Perhaps the village offered better work prospects for the young men. It may also be the case that John Goldthorp, as a land valuer, was able to point them towards business opportunities through knowing when and where new buildings were to be erected.

Alternatively there could have been a psychological or emotional reason. Were George's brothers aware that he was finding it increasingly difficult to live so close to the murder scene? If he was also having to hide what he knew (or suspected) about Brearley, Stott and Ramsden, this could have put him under great stress. What better solution than to get away from Clifton and start anew?

By the 1851 census George Pratt had put an even greater distance between himself and Clifton. From Rastrick he moved alone to the town of Huddersfield. There he lived as a lodger at a house in Charles Street. His status as boarder or lodger continued in the town for the next twenty years.

His last appearance in a census, however, shows yet another move. In 1881 we find him living in Stockport, Cheshire. Aged sixty-six, he is still recorded as a leather currier, still a boarder, still unmarried. George seems to have lived an itinerant life, constantly on the move, constantly unsettled, in a manner unusual for a man with his family background. Something, it seems, was eating at George Pratt.

# CHAPTER 20

# I'm following in Father's footsteps

After moving to Rastrick, Joseph Stott's life settled into an unexceptional groove. By 1841 he was married to Elizabeth Caygill, a dressmaker, and the couple had a one-year-old son, William. The family lived at Rastrick Common. With George Pratt's home less than a mile away, they must have passed each other quite often, though to what extent they kept in contact we do not know.

Over the next two decades Joseph's family grew with the addition of seven daughters, and by 1861 the family had moved to a new address in Lillands Lane, probably needing more space for their large brood.

Surprisingly, Joseph's only son, William, did not follow him into currying or any of the connected leather occupations, such as shoemaking or glove making, becoming instead an iron moulder. Although the currying trade declined at the start of the twentieth century, it was much in demand through the nineteenth, so William's choice of a different trade is unexpected, especially as he was the only son and would eventually have inherited his father's business. Of course there is the possibility that Joseph's business did not thrive sufficiently for his son to join it: there is no evidence that Joseph took on apprentices, evidently lacking Ramsden's drive and ambition.

Joseph's last appearance in a census is in 1881, still living with his wife and family in Lillands Lane and still a currier. After the tragedy and high drama of the Clifton Wood murder, he lived out his days without connection to further scandal. If he did play a part in the murder of Liz Rayner, it seems the fates allowed it to pass with little in the way of revenge.

John Brearley was not so fortunate.

*　　*　　*

*11 August 1839*

*It is an overcast day. Fat, green-black clouds squat on the distant skyline over Brighouse, giving the light a sickly cast. The air is oppressive with the threat of a summer storm, and as Thomas Ramsden walks up the path to Hartshead church he pulls at his shirt collar where beads of sweat are trickling down his neck. Beside him walks his wife, Ann. Despite the humidity, she appears coolly graceful in a new sprigged cotton gown and straw bonnet. As they approach the small group of people outside the church, she slips a proprietary hand into the crook of his arm.*

*At the church door stands John Brearley with his wife, Sarah Ann, and their children – two-year-old Thomas Henry, Ramsden's namesake, a lively, sturdy child with impossibly mischievous blue eyes, and Benjamin, the two-month-old baby, soundly asleep in his mother's arms.*

*'Morning, Thomas. Morning, Ann,' calls John. After years of feeling like a servant he now enjoys the status of first-name terms.*

*Thomas and Ann nod and smile their hellos.*

*'Now then, Sarah Ann,' says Ramsden in playful tone, placing an arm around her, 'you look as fresh and fair as a Golcar lily, and that's no word of a lie.'*

*Brearley looks away to hide his annoyance. What is Ramsden playing at? The man simply can't help himself, can he? What is he now – almost forty? And still he can't stop prowling round attractive females. John is annoyed but determined to hide it, unlike Ann Ramsden, whose serene mask slips momentarily to reveal a spark of anger and humiliation at her husband's predatory charm. To distract herself she reaches out to take baby Benjamin from his mother and proceeds to coo over him.*

*'He looks well,' she says, adding with more grace than she feels, 'And so do you, Sarah Ann.' This is not entirely true. Sarah Ann is pretty in the same delicate manner as her infant son, but the shadows beneath her eyes are deep and hint at a more ominous cause than the loss of sleep a new baby brings.*

*Little Thomas toddles over to his adult namesake and lifts his arms to him, an invitation impossible to resist. Ramsden swings him up and tosses him into the air, making the child shriek and giggle.*

*'Tom, don't get the child giddy or the vicar'll be annoyed,' warns Ann.*

*At that very moment the vicar appears behind them. 'Is everyone here?' he asks without greeting. 'Shall we begin?'*

*The Reverend Mr Atkinson still finds himself overcome with nerves when confronted by Ramsden and his ex-apprentices, but is unaware how painfully obvious this is. Inside he still simmers with the injustice of it all. How can the Lord allow such black-hearted villains to thrive? As he summons the group into the cool interior of the church and leads them to the font, Ramsden and Brearley exchange a look that is part amusement, part triumph.*

\*     \*     \*

John Brearley married Sarah Ann Green, daughter of John Green, a farm labourer, on 17 April 1836. It was obviously a hasty marriage as their first child, Thomas Henry, was baptised on 10 July, less than three months after the wedding. Just how readily John entered into the marriage with her is unknown, but it does present another intriguing possibility: was John already seeing Sarah Ann Green when Elizabeth Rayner announced she was pregnant? Two points lend support to this idea.

The first is that after the speculation and rumour surrounding Liz's death there must have been deep mistrust of Ramsden and his apprentices, with Brearley especially under suspicion. What father and mother would happily agree to their daughter being courted by a suspected killer? If the young man was already known to them, however, they might be more inclined to dismiss the rumours as unfounded gossip and allow the courtship to go ahead.

The second point is that if Brearley was in love with Sarah Ann and hoped to make her his wife, a pregnant ex-girlfriend was a serious obstacle in his path. As Elizabeth's pregnancy progressed he would have come under increasing pressure to marry her, which would have caused mounting frustration and resentment, especially given his uncertainty over whether the child was his. Passion for Sarah Ann might have been sufficient to tip him from anger and resentment into murder.

\*     \*     \*

*Sarah Ann Green can hardly believe her ears. She stops and turns to face Martha Wood and Jane Lockwood, walking a few paces behind her.*

*'What did you just say?' she asks, anger sharpening her voice.*

*'You heard,' answers Martha. 'Your chap's a bloody murderer and he needs . . .' But before she can complete the sentence Sarah Ann is flying at her, hands grabbing for the girl's hair.*

*Although she's slight, almost frail, her fury propels her like a missile and her enemy is on the ground before she knows what is happening. Martha screams as her attacker's fingernails rake down her cheeks.*

*'Don't you ever say that again!' hisses Sarah Ann.*

*'Jane! Get her off me!' Martha begs. But Jane is so shocked by the onslaught that she simply stands watching, in open-mouthed horror.*

*Sarah Ann has Martha pinned to the ground, her hands round the girl's neck. 'Don't ever say owt like that again, else it'll be the last thing you do say.'*

*'Hey! Break it up! Break it up!' The parish constable, Charles Ramsden, appears from the doorway of the Black Horse and pulls Sarah Ann off Martha, expending rather more effort in the process than he expected.*

*'She attacked her!' cries Jane. 'She's mad!'*

*With the constable's substantial presence a barrier between them, the girls stand glaring at each other, Martha protectively covering her scratched cheek.*

*'Brawling like a pair of washer women! Get off with you before I think about opening the stocks,' warns the constable.*

*Martha and Jane need no extra bidding and scurry off down the lane, casting backward glares at Sarah Ann.*

*Charles Ramsden shakes his head pityingly. Whatever does this waif of a lass want with Brearley? Anyone with any sense must see that for all the lad's cool manner he's shot through with temper. 'Leave Brearley to fight his own battles,' he advises.*

*'He can't fight what he doesn't know, can he? I'm sick of all the tittle-tattle in this village. You can't stir without some busybody making it their business. John's the kindest, gentlest lad I know. He'd not hurt a fly. But I suppose you've got it in for him an' all.'*

*'Go on, lass. Get yourself home before there's more bother.'*

*Sarah Ann picks up her shawl, shakes the dust and dirt from it, then sets off down the lane.*

*The constable watches her go, shaking his head sadly. He wonders what it is about John Brearley that elicits such loyalty. He wonders, too, why the nice girls always choose bad lads. And Brearley – well, that lad is dyed-in-the-wool bad.*

\*     \*     \*

If John Brearley found happiness with Sarah Ann, it was short lived. She was buried on 13 January 1840 at the age of twenty-five, her death leaving him with four-year-old Thomas Henry and seven-month-old Benjamin. It is no surprise, then, to find him in the 1841 and 1851 censuses living with his in-laws, John and Sarah Green, at Haley Cottage.

During the years between the two censuses circumstances improved for the Greens. From being described simply as an agricultural labourer in 1841, by 1851 John Green had become a farmer of 16 acres. John Brearley is still described as a currier, and his sons Thomas and Benjamin are recorded respectively as an apprentice currier and a scholar. Exactly how the Greens' fortunes improved so dramatically over those ten years cannot be readily identified, but there is surely the possibility of help from a certain Thomas Ramsden, who by this time must have been at the height of his wealth and influence.

By 1861, though, John Brearley's in-laws are shown to be living alone. John and his sons are not recorded in the census at all. Their omission may be because the 1861 census for the Halifax area is incomplete. Fortunately their location is revealed in 1863 through newspaper articles in the *Halifax Courier* and the *Halifax Guardian,* reporting the theft of nine butts of leather from John's workshop in Back Rhodes Street, Halifax. It is of particular interest to note that the employee suspected of stealing the leather went by the surname Ramsden. (The two newspapers do not agree on his first name: the *Courier* refers to him as John while the *Guardian* calls him Daniel.) Documentary evidence proves the thieving employee cannot have been Thomas Ramsden's son John (who was living with his widowed mother in Clifton by 1861), but it seems likely he was related to some degree. Presumably here is yet another example of the economic closeness of the Brearley and Ramsden families.

The *Halifax Guardian* report informs us that the thief 'went into the cellar under pretence of sharpening an instrument used in the trade and it was supposed he left the door open. Not appearing at his work as usual, suspicion fell on him and information was given to the police. In the meantime one of the sons of Mr Brearley went to California and asked if Ramsden was coming to his work and the reply was – yes, he will be down directly. The police went up to the house and made a search, finding the whole lot of leather in the house but Ramsden had gone.'

In the 1871 census John Brearley is no longer resident in Back Rhodes Street. His sons, both married with young children, are still working as curriers – Benjamin on Back Rhodes Street, probably at his father's old premises, and Thomas Henry round the corner on Rhodes Street. John's absence suggests he died between 1863 and 1871, but he had left his sons well equipped to make good. And already in 1871 this is exactly what Thomas Henry is doing: at the age of only thirty-four he is recorded as a master currier, employing eight men and three boys. Living with him, his wife and four children are also two servants, one a female domestic and the other a currier's servant. The occupations of their neighbours include a glover, a solicitor and a leather merchant, suggesting an affluent area of town. Thomas Henry's drive and ambition reflects that of his father and his father's master.

His brother, by contrast, does not seem to have inherited the drive and ambition of his father, and Benjamin is recorded as a solitary worker employing neither men nor servants. He will have fared well enough, however, as a skilled craftsman, and John must have felt by the end of his life that whatever else he had done in his time on earth, he had not let his lads down.

CHAPTER 21

# And with thee fade into the forest dim

*Stockport, Cheshire, 1881*

    *George Pratt looks round the mean little attic room he calls home and takes another swig of beer straight from the bottle. Rust-coloured fingers of damp streak the chimney breast and the faded wallpaper gives off a musty, sour smell. It's chilly and he ought to set a fire but he's that weary he can't be bothered – the counterpane will keep the worst of the cold at bay.*

    *From downstairs the tempting aroma of stew wafts up and tickles his nostrils. Mrs Jameson is cooking the evening meal and he could join her and her husband if he wanted to, but that's not his way. She'll bring a plate up for him later, leaving it outside his door. The Jamesons are a right enough couple – he's an overlooker at the cotton mill, she keeps house – and the two other boarders, Archibald and Sam, seem decent enough lads, but . . . well, they're not his folk, not by blood or place, and frankly he can't be arsed to act all polite and interested in them when the truth is he doesn't give a damn.*

    *Suddenly the room feels as if it's shrinking, suffocating him. He throws off the counterpane and lurches to the skylight window, which he pushes open to breathe in the evening air. He stares across the rooftops of houses, churches and factories, and feels perplexed by time and place. What is he doing here? Whoever would have thought he'd end up so far from God's own county? Not him, that's for sure. These are his third lodgings in Stockport and he knows they won't be his last, because no matter where he goes she always finds him in the end.*

    *He'd thought at first that a new county might make a difference – that*

107

*despite her unnerving ability to track him down, Cheshire's unfamiliar landscapes might outfox her. No such luck. She allus finds him. She storms his room like an icy blast and stands beside him, the wide wound to her throat like a ghastly leer. She says nothing and does nothing – she only watches him, a mocking smile in her eyes. So this bit of breathing space here in Swallow Street is only temporary. She'll find him again. It's just a matter of time.*

*The truth is, though, he's absolutely jiggered with running away. In the past he's tried ignoring her, threatening her – God love him – he's even tried to grab her. Now if that's not the act of a madman he doesn't know what is . . . but no matter what he does, once she's found him she's as constant as his shadow.*

*Perhaps it's time to stop running.*

*   *   *

In many ways George Pratt's character and circumstances highlight him as prime suspect: there is the nipping incident, his chaotic statement before the coroner, his inability to settle anywhere after the murder and his continuing single state. Why, then, does my theory find him innocent of involvement? If, as this argument postulates, the murder was a result of a conspiracy between Ramsden, Brearley and Stott, they would not want to involve more people than necessary – especially George Pratt, who comes across very strongly as an outsider.

To recap: it is George who contradicts some of Brearley, Rachel and Ramsden's evidence; it is he who draws the attention of the court to Rachel's pregnancy and Ramsden's marital strife; it is he whose invitation to Brearley on New Year's Eve is refused; it is he who lives outside the Ramsden household. If he had suspicions about the others, this would put him in a difficult situation: tell, and risk a not guilty verdict against his master and colleagues, or stay silent and wrestle with his conscience for ever more.

*   *   *

*Clifton, 31 December 1882*

*The weak light of a winter afternoon is surrendering to the shades of dusk. After the breath-stealing hike up Clifton Common (surely steeper than he remembers) George Pratt moves slowly along Town Gate, hat pulled down low over his face to avoid recognition. As he greets each new landmark of his youth the years seem to retreat. This is his first return to the village in over forty years, and though much is as it was there are remarkable changes too. For a start, an imposing Anglican church dedicated to St John the Evangelist now stands with serene pride on West Cross Close and, not to be outdone by their Anglican brethren, the Methodists have erected a robust chapel on the site where William Fearnley and John Green's cottages once stood. The chapel's existence brings a wry smile to his face. Old Sir George Armytage must be turning in his grave at the upstart's presence.*

*Further down the street the Black Bull's windows run with condensation, while the shouts and laughter of men released from work spill out to the street. For a moment he pauses, tempted by the lure of ale, but then notices a face staring curiously at him from the doorway, which is enough to set him on his way again.*

*Passing Ramsden's workshops is the hardest part. It fair takes the wind out of his sails when up near the barn he sees a strongly built man carrying a pile of hides towards the currying shed. The energetic movements and sharply angled jaw confirm the man as a Ramsden, most likely one of Thomas's sons, but the unexpected likeness makes George's stomach lurch and roll, forcing him to grasp the wall for support. Time has executed a series of backflips, sending him giddy.*

*Fifty years ago this very day, almost to the minute, he was packing up his tools, looking forward to a night on the ale with his friends. He can still recall how sluffed he'd felt at Brearley's refusal to go to Brighouse with him. Stott he didn't mind about so much – too quiet a lad for a right good night. But Brearley . . . Brearley was special. Brearley was everything George admired in a man – tall, firm muscled, hard as nails and charming as a lass when it served his purpose. No wonder Thomas Ramsden favoured him. They were two of a kind – clever and ambitious enough to smash any obstacles in their paths without a second thought.*

*Of course he knew something was going on from the way Brearley and Ramsden had started like guilty kids when he walked into the mistal. At first he'd suspected they were talking about him – he wasn't as quick as the other two. But the next day, when they found Liz's body, he knew at once what they'd been plotting.*

*George feels feverish and a bit dizzy. Never mind. Tonight he'll have it out with her once and for all, and that will be that. If she wants him to speak out he will. With Thomas and John mouldering in the ground it's not as if there'll be a trial, so where's the harm?*

*By now dusk has sunk into night. The Black Horse looks much the same, although he notes the name of a new licensee above the door: Samuel Clayton. The voices from inside are, if anything, even more raucous than at the Black Bull, and tonight noises have a metallic sound to him, as if their edges have been sharpened on a grinder. He covers his ears and hurries past.*

*With only the faintest sliver of moonlight to guide him, George makes his way carefully along the narrow path at the edge of the wood. The branches of the trees reach out, welcoming him home.*

*To his surprise he does not have to seek her out, for there she is, leaning against the gateway to the wood, a teasing smile on her face.*

*'Evening, George,' she says. She extends a small, almost transparent hand towards him.*

*George hesitates. 'So you've finally decided to talk to me. What do you want?' he asks.*

*It would be all too easy to let this shade fool him into believing she's real. He must keep a grip on himself. This isn't Liz Rayner – it's a vision, a ghost, something from his imaginings. But the image is so vivid, every little movement an echo of the flesh and blood girl who lived, loved and died here fifty years ago.*

*'You think I was a lot to blame,' says Liz, jumping nimbly onto a tree stump. She smiles down at him, her glorious red halo of hair like a cloud around the moon. 'You think I was hedging my bets with John, waiting to see if I could trap Ramsden first. You're right. I didn't want to end up like our Sarah: no husband, no support and a baby to care for. I had to make sure there'd be somebody there for us.'*

*'But you must have known Ramsden would never leave his wife,' says George. 'Why not just settle for Brearley?'*

*'It wasn't that simple. John was seeing Sarah Ann – he was head over heels for her. Would **you** want someone who was pining for someone else? Course not. So Brearley wasn't what I wanted – more of a last resort if I couldn't get Ramsden to see things my way.'*

*The audacity of Liz's plan astonishes George. 'Whatever were you thinking of? You don't corner a man like Ramsden.'*

*Liz laughs shortly. 'I know that now! But I wasn't asking him to leave his wife and marry me. I'd have been happy enough with money for me and the child. Might have worked an' all, except Rachel had the same idea. Only she had an advantage over me: Ramsden were a bit in love with her.'*

*'So you were the jig in the bed.'*

*Liz nods and smiles broadly. 'Aye, that's me – an itch he couldn't scratch.'*

*George shakes his head. 'And you didn't want to wed Brearley 'cos of Sarah Ann. But . . . I thought you were just leading Brearley a merry dance.'*

*'Aye. And you couldn't let that happen to your precious friend. I was the mad, bad cow and you were going to save him from me. And that nip bloody hurt! Oh, George, it's no use looking like that. We all knew. You'd have given your soul to the devil for him.'*

*'Brearley was my friend. You try and help your friends out,' George mutters defensively.*

*Taking no notice of his discomfort, Liz continues. 'Anyroad, at first it was the two of them against each other. Ramsden had the whip hand over John, what with being his master an' all, and he did his best to push us into getting wed. But when it came down to it, I thought why settle for the servant when I might have the master? So I made it plain I'd point the finger at Ramsden if he didn't agree to take care of me. And Rachel said the same.'*

*'So you thought you'd got it all tied up,' sneers George. 'Came loose pretty quickly, though, didn't it?'*

*Liz smiles ruefully. 'It did that. You see, it never occurred to me any of 'em was brazen or wicked enough to kill a lass.'*

*'And Stott? I may be miles out, but I reckon he was in on it.'*

*'Didn't have much choice, did he?'*

*'Meaning?'*

*'Don't tell me you didn't know! Did your brothers never let on? Joseph Stott was the leader of the poaching gang. A natural hunter. Our Robert told me Joe could stalk deer like an invisible man. They were doing right well – making more than a wire drawer makes, that's for sure. They sold the hides to Ramsden and he passed 'em off as cow. If there was a man knew what was going off in Clifton that man was Tom Ramsden.'*

*George feels dazed. 'Well, well. I could never work it out before. I'd never have guessed Stott was in on the snecking. He were such a quiet lad . . .'*

*'Isn't it them you've got to watch?' says Liz, meaningfully.*

*Suddenly the teasing Liz is gone: in her place a quivering fury. 'Did you think I wouldn't have fought for my life? For my baby's life? Did you think they wouldn't have known that? Well, it took two of them to do it – Brearley and Stott – the two of them to drag me into the wood. I begged* them and begged them. What had my baby done to hurt them? But they didn't care. Not them to blame, the master's orders. This is from Thomas Ramsden – that's what Brearley said when he pulled the knife across my throat – from Thomas Ramsden. And you such a coward as daren't tell a soul, no matter what wrong was done to me!'

George wants to protest, to point out he was only trying to protect his brothers, her brother too if it comes to that, but he can't seem to get his breath. It's as if a 10 ton weight is pressing on his chest, while a mean, cold fist squeezes his heart.

Liz steps nearer, her face so close to his he can smell the mouldering earth in her breath. 'It's too late, George. May God forgive you, for I never can.'

And with that she turns, her form misting into nothingness beneath the branches of the dark, still wood . . .

# Degrees of separation

Research into family history frequently unearths fascinating and unexpected information. Sometimes ancestors emerge into the light, glowing with the saintliness of their deeds; others skulk in the shadows of black-hearted villainy; while the majority leave behind impressions of lives more ordinary, but well lived. A life cut short, especially by murder, always casts a melancholic shadow of could-have-beens.

I first heard about the murder of Elizabeth Rayner from my grandmother, Phyllis Depledge, née Sheard. Her great-grandfather was Elizabeth's brother John, thus making him my great-grandfather times three, and Elizabeth Rayner my great-aunt times four. The story, told with a keen sense of drama by my gran, was an intriguing tale that raised a whole host of questions. About ten years ago I decided to try and find some hard evidence to either support or demolish what I suspected might have been produced from my grandmother's fertile imagination.

My suspicions were wrong. To my surprise, reports in three editions of the *Halifax Guardian and Huddersfield and Bradford Advertiser* gave information that supported what she had told me. I dug around a bit more, but for a while the trail appeared to have gone cold.

Late in 2009 a work colleague, Paul Weatherhead, discovered that depositions from the coroner's inquiry were available at the National Archives. I immediately chased these up and was astonished at the insights they gave, allowing me to research the murder in much greater depth and develop a theory about what happened. Genealogical research also produced surprises.

Perhaps the greatest of these was the discovery that not only was I related to Elizabeth Rayner but also, and more directly, descended from the apprentice Joseph Stott through his daughter, Nancy. Nancy married Thomas Flintoff and their daughter Lily was my grandmother's mother, making Joseph Stott my great-grandfather times three.

A further connection is that Joseph's brother Jonas had a child called John, who was the great-grandfather times three of Elizabeth Stott, who married my mother's brother, Ronald Horne. By this point I suspect readers can hear the banjos playing . . .

My theory about the murder of Elizabeth Rayner may or may not be near the mark. Without the benefit of hard evidence, an incontrovertible verdict cannot be reached. But this, in part, is the fascination of the case. In conclusion, I hope this book achieves three things; firstly, I hope it interests and intrigues its audience; secondly, that it provokes discussion and further theories about the case; and finally, that it stands as a memorial to a young woman whose tragic fate was almost forgotten.

*Visit my Blog: http://borrowersofthenight.blogspot.com*
*Follow me on Twitter: http://twitter.com/annabest1*

# Depositions

Depositions taken at Clifton, 4th January 1833 upon an inquest on the body of Elizabeth Rayner

**Samuel Brearley** of Clifton, aged 14 years, saith, I was playing with Simeon and John Rayner in Clifton wood on Tuesday afternoon. I saw something laid there. Simeon went up and he said, "It is our Liz." I went up too but I did not know her.

She was laid on her belly, arms crossed and her head was upon her arms. Her head was uphill. There was some blood a yard above her in the wood – some on her back fair across her shoulders a great deal. I saw no knife, scissors or razor near her – I came into town and told it directly. Her shoe toes had gone right into the ground – the ground was all leaves and I could not tell whether anybody else had been there. I could not see any footsteps. I did not search for anything. Her hair had fallen down into her neck but it was not very rough. I knew her when she was living – her legs were bare but her gown was not torn at the back – it was covered with blood at the back.

Samuel Brearley

**Thomas Ramsden of Clifton,** aforesaid currier, saith, the last time I saw Elizabeth Rayner is three weeks ago in West Gate in Clifton. I had some conversation with her. She came to tell me that Benjamin Glover was going to be married that day and he wished me to go. She has been at my house since; I heard her but I did not see her. It was the day but one after Christmas Day. She has not been at our house except the above day, and another when I was from home, for the last three months during which time I have not seen her more than three or four times and not to hold conversation with her. I was at this house (The Black Horse) on Monday near two o'clock in the afternoon. I left and went to collect money as Surveyor of the Highways. I returned to this house about seven o'clock. I remained a quarter of an hour and got a gill of beer. I then went home, went to see what the lads had been doing. George Pratt and John Brearley were sat opposite each other. They had a band fixed, playing at Snatch Apples. Then I left my house. I went down Sheep Cote Lane and Coal Pit Lane about half past seven to Brighouse. I had in a way promised David Collings to go. I got home about 1o'clock. I got to the Anchor about 8 o'clock. I stayed there till nearly eleven. I was in company with John Thompson and George Widdop and Samuel Lister. I was with the last named all the time. I then went to Mrs Waddington's till between twelve and one. I then came home by Clifton Common and down the town alone. I met no one. I never heard of her being lost till I heard of her death. I slept at home that night. I rose at eight the following morning. Rachel Brooke left my Service on account of some jealousy of my wife that I was too free with her. I never had any connection in my life with the deceased, nor did I ever ask her to have any.

Thomas Ramsden


**Rachel Brooke** of Clifton, single woman, saith, I live at the Alms Houses in Clifton. I was a particular friend of the deceased. We have gone together for two or three years.

I was not at Glover's on Monday night last. The last time I saw her was on Sunday night at our house. She left about 10 o'clock. She went away by herself. There were no young men in our house that night. She agreed to meet at the Alms Houses on the Monday night. I did not meet her because I had not done my work at Thomas Ramsden's. I was washing and mangling clothes there – I left about 10 o'clock. When I left, all the family were in except Thomas Ramsden and John Brearley. John Brearley left the house about half past seven in the evening. Thomas Ramsden left home about noon and came back around seven o'clock, then went out again and he did not come back whilst I stayed. I lived two years and a half at Ramsden's as servant and left there for ill health. My Master and Mistress had some quarrels about me as it was reported he was too intimate with me. The deceased told me frequently she was with child by John Brearley. I know him very well. He is Thomas Ramsden's apprentice. I have seen them together many a time in Sheep Cote Lane, New England End, and many a place. It was always in the evening, perhaps nine or ten and at a holiday time half past ten. George Pratt keeps company with me. The deceased has slept once or twice with me at Thomas Ramsden's . Once in coming from Oakenshaw Fair, Elizabeth and me and Martha Walker went to the fair and Thomas Ramsden came home with us. When I left Ramsden's last Monday night, Joseph Ramsden, brother of Thomas, and George, son of Thomas, went with me nearly home. We went on Sheep Cote Lane. I went into the house directly. The lads went back. We neither met nor passed anyone. I heard nothing in the wood as I passed on the lane. I never heard George Pratt say anything against Elizabeth Rayner – I remember Pratt nipping Elizabeth but I don't know the cause. It went black. Elizabeth told me she would not have cried out if he had nipped the piece out. I never heard Elizabeth kept company with anybody but Brearley. They have been sweethearts for two or three years. Brearley told me a few nights since that he was the father of Elizabeth's child but he once before told me he had not got it all himself. Elizabeth Rayner frequently came to see me when I was at Ramsden's – she was 15 or 16 weeks gone with child. When I heard Elizabeth was dead in the wood I screamed and went to her immediately. Brearley was very kind to Elizabeth and I never heard him say anything against her. She was a very cheerful girl and has never been low spirited about the child. She has not worn a pocket for a good few weeks.

X Rachel Brooke her mark


**Robert Rayner** of Clifton, aforesaid wiredrawer, saith, the deceased was my sister. She was at Hannah Glover's last Monday night at the Alms Houses about nine o'clock playing at Blindy Buff. I went in and said to her, "I think it will be as well for thee to be at home. Go and see if my mother does not want thee to do something this evening." She went off. She said, "If she does not want me, I shall come again," and she would lay on me. I said I thought she would be too little – this passed in a joking way – I saw her leave but did not see her again that evening. She was in good spirits. My mother did not send me, and I sent her home of myself. They were all girls in the houses, no men. My sister had kept company with John Brearley, an apprentice with Thomas Ramsden of Clifton. He never came to our house and I never saw them together. My sister was with child but I don't know who by. I never asked her.

I only stayed about five minutes after my sister. I left the Alms Houses in company with five young women and went on to Brighouse and it was twelve o'clock before I got home. Our family was all up but my sister had not come in. She had not been in the habit of staying out all night but has come as late as twelve o'clock at night.

I went to seek her on Tuesday morning about ten o'clock. I went to the Alms Houses but I did not go into Clifton Wood. I went to my uncle John Rayner's at the top of Clifton and when I was coming from there I was told she was found in Clifton Wood with her throat cut. I did not go into Clifton Wood to see her. I have seen her since she was dead since she was got home. When I went to Brighouse from the Alms Houses I passed down Coal Pit Lane. I did not pass by the Quarry and had my shoes on then that I have now.

X Robert Rayner his mark


**Elizabeth Rayner** of Clifton, wife of William Rayner and mother of the deceased, saith, my daughter left my house about seven o'clock on Monday night last. She came to me in some time after at Widow Oldfield's and asked me if I wanted her and I told her I did not want her. She said Robert had said that she (the witness) wanted me – she was to come home. I told her it was only his nonsense – this was about nine o'clock. She was not angry. I left her in Oldfield's and we never saw her alive afterwards. She never told me she was with child but I let her know we knew. She did not tell me who by and I never asked her. I don't know how far she was gone. I told her of it nearly two months ago. I don't know who she kept company with. She has been out as late as twelve or one o'clock at night she was mostly at Tom Ramsden's. She stayed twice out all night, and then she slept at Richard Walker's at Oakenshaw and the following night she slept at Tom Ramsden's – this was last Oakenshaw Fair. Last Monday night I went to bed about twelve o'clock and left the door open for her being holiday time. I thought she would be coming. The morning after, around eleven o'clock I think, I went to Glover's at the Alms Houses and searched other places to find her but no one could tell me anything of her.

X Elizabeth Rayner her mark

*The clerk probably meant, 'She said that Robert said that I (the witness) wanted her', as otherwise what is recorded does not make sense.*

**Abigail Oldfield,** of Clifton, the aforesaid widow, saith, the deceased came to my house on Monday evening last about nine o'clock. She was by herself alone. She did not stay many minutes. She did not sit down. No one went out with her. She was in good spirits but vexed with her brother for fetching her and said she would go back to Hannah Glover's and she would not come again. This was the last time I saw her alive. I knew she was with child. She frequently came into my house sitting a bit.

X Abigail Oldfield her mark

**Elizabeth Brooke** of Clifton, aforesaid single woman, saith, I live at the Alms Houses in Clifton next door but one to Hannah Glover's. The deceased was playing and very cheerful at Hannah Glover's last Monday night. She was in my house about seven o'clock and we all went in together to Glover's. She left Glover's about five minutes to nine o'clock. She went out alone and we asked her if she would come again and she said she would if her mother did not want her. We left soon after and Robert went with some young women to Brighouse. (She had no comb in her hair.) My daughter Rachel and her were great friends – they were like sisters – I knew she was with child and when she told of it she neither wished it was or was not . She was a cheerful girl naturally. No one ever saw her low spirited.

I know John Brearley kept company with her. I have often seen them together in the daytime but not in the night.

X Elizabeth Brooke her mark


**Hannah Glover** of Clifton, widow, saith, I live at the Alms Houses. The deceased was at my house last Monday evening. She was very cheerful. Her brother fetched her and said that her mother wanted her. She said she would come back if her mother did not want her. She and some other young women were playing at thimble. I heard her say she had no pocket on. She has sometimes called at my house. Five weeks ago this evening she was at my house and George Pratt, who is an apprentice at Thomas Ramsden's, was there. He nipped (pinched) her left arm. It turned black and yellow but she did not call out. She left before him. I asked him the day after why he had nipped her and he said it was nothing to me and abused me sadly.

X Hannah Glover her mark


**Joseph Stott** of Clifton, currier, saith, I live with Thomas Ramsden of Clifton. I am apprentice to him. I was standing opposite this house (the Black Horse) Monday night about ten minutes past nine o'clock. Elizabeth Rayner, the deceased, passed close by me and I said to her, "Hello Elizabeth," and she said, "Hello Joseph," and went on towards Sheep Cote Lane. She went by herself. I could see her go forwards about twenty yards. She answered me in good spirits. She was at my Master's house a week since last Wednesday. She was talking to Rachel Brooke, the servant. My Master was not at home on Monday afternoon nor on Tuesday. I have heard John Brearley say that Elizabeth Rayner was with child by him but I never heard of its being any other person's. John Brearley sleeps with me. He slept with me last Monday evening. He came inside at ten minutes before ten o'clock. I guess this and cannot tell to a minute or two. Brearley and me went to bed that night ten minutes past ten. My Master was not at home when I went to bed.

Joseph Stott

**John Brearley** of Clifton, currier, saith, I live with Thomas Ramsden and am apprenticed currier. I knew Elizabeth Rayner – we were sweethearts. She was with child by me. The last time I saw her was on Sunday night last. George Pratt was with me. At Coppera's hill we passed on the road but we did not speak. We were friendly for anything I knew – we frequently passed without speaking. We met at different places. She came to my master's sometimes. I am eighteen years old – I have known and kept company with her two or three years. I have never been out late at night. I have never said that my master has had connection with her. I never blamed anybody for the child. I did say to Rachel Brooke that I had not got all the child myself.

I was at Clifton last Monday all day. I gave over work at dark about half past four. I stayed in the house till within five or ten minutes of nine o'clock. I came out with Stott and Pratt. Pratt left me in the fold and wished me to go to Brighouse. He left me and I came forwards with Joseph Stott into the street to the bottom of John Brodon's Field. I went into Joseph Pratt's and stopped till half past 9. Charles Pratt and me came out and went as far as to Thomas Dixon's and ? to the Black Horse door stones at a quarter to ten o'clock and I then went home and met Joseph Stott locking the stable of my Master and we both went into the house together. It wanted 5 or 10 minutes to 10 o'clock. I went to bed 10 minutes past 10. My Master was not at home when I went to bed. I have been in Clifton wood with Elizabeth Rayner two or three times but I have not been with her there since she was with child. I was by Sam Clayton when I heard of her death with a band of music.

My Master did not dine with us on Tuesday. He was with us upstairs in the morning. He was at breakfast. I went to see the deceased yesterday. I did not go before because William Rayner said it was all me or my Master and he would have us taken up. I did not go into the wood because I did not like to see such a sight. I was with the band at the time. Rachel Brooke left our house before 10. We played at Blindy Buff during the evening for some time before milking time and after that at snatch apples.

John Brearley

**George Pratt** of Clifton, aforesaid currier, saith, I am apprentice to Thomas Ramsden. I last saw the deceased about six o'clock on Monday evening at the town end by herself – she passed me – she was going towards Sheep Cote Lane. She came to Ramsden's sometimes. I do not sleep at Ramsden's. I heard of her being missing on Tuesday noon. I was in the Black Horse just getting a pint of ale and I heard she was dead in the wood. I ran down – she was laid on her belly with her arms folded under her head. There was blood around her neck. I came away directly. She was not turned over. She had not been touched up to that time. I kept company with Rachel Brooke above a year ago. I was once at Glover's with the deceased a month or better ago. I joked her, she would not speak to me. I squeezed her a bit in my nonsense. I did nip her on the left arm but not violently – it was on the left arm. I saw Brearley last Monday night. We left together. I wanted him to go to Brighouse but he would not go. I got home at twelve o'clock. James Crabtree and Joseph Hirst came home with me. We had been at John Goldthorp's. We returned up Coal Pit Lane and passed on Sheep Cote Lane. We neither saw nor heard anything of the deceased. It was a fine night. I left my work at half past four – I played at Blindy Buff with Rachel Brooke, Brearley and Stott and one of my master's brothers. We left Rachel Brooke there – she had been washing. I had seen my master about three o'clock that afternoon. I cannot say whether it was morning or the afternoon. He was at home on Tuesday morning. I cannot say what time – about 8 o'clock. I saw him coming over the Black Horse door stones that afternoon. Rachel Brooke said to me the last time she came to my Master's that I must have her child – My Master and Mistress did not agree very well about Rachel as there was a deal of talk about her and my Master. We did not play at any other games than Blindy Buff at my Master's. They had milked before I left. I believe Brearley milked. Master came into the mistal. I have heard Brearley say that somebody joined him at the child. I have seen Walsh's Lad with her at the wood end.

George Pratt


**Luke Hoyles** of Mirfield, surgeon
**John Collings Leadbetter** of Mirfield, surgeon, saith, I was called in by the constable of Clifton yesterday to examine the body of the

deceased. I found an incised wound from 2 inches and a half to 3 inches long. It separated the trachea and integuments, leaving a small part of the back part of the trachea. The small blood vessels externally and internally were divided. She died from suffocation of blood and the wound together. I cannot say by what sort of instrument it was done. I cannot say whether it was done with the right or left hand. Under the left ear were two abrasions of the skin about an inch long, each done by some rough instrument or falling upon a stone. On the forefinger of the left hand is a cut by a sharp instrument and the nail is black. There is a mark on the left cheek which shows a blueness as if a blow had been given.

Luke Hoyle
John Collings Leadbetter

Verdict: wilful murder against person or persons unknown

# Sir George's letter

*Kirklees nr Leeds*
*Jan 31ˢᵗ 1833*

*My Lord,*
    *I beg leave to trouble yr Lordship with this letter, to inform you that a most cruel murder was committed on the 31st of December last or on the 1st of January in a wood called Clifton wood in the township of Clifton in the West Riding of the county of York and belonging to me within a short distance of my mansion house at Kirklees – I have sent for yr Lordship's inspection the depositions taken before the coroner's court, by which you will find a verdict was found by a jury of wilful murder against a person or persons unknown. Every investigation on my part as a magistrate and by the inhabitants of Clifton has been made, and I am sorry to say that we cannot as yet find any clues to lead to the discovery of the murderer Therefore, this dreadful affair at present rests unresolved. A reward has been offered by myself and the inhabitants of Clifton of one hundred pounds. If your Lordship thinks that an additional reward from his Majesty may lead to a discovery of this most cruel murderer, the inhabitants of Clifton and myself will most gratefully acknowledge his Majesty's condescension in complying with our request for whatever sum he may think proper to grant.*
    *I have the honour to remain yr Lordship's most obedient humble servant.*

**Geo: Armytage**

# APPENDIX 3

# Newspaper articles

From the *Halifax Guardian and Huddersfield and Bradford Advertiser*

## Saturday 5 January 1833
On Tuesday afternoon Inst, an unmarried woman, about 20 years of age, named Elizabeth Rayner, was found in Clifton Wood, about 200 yards from her own residence, with her throat cut. She was last seen alive on the preceding evening and was in a state of pregnancy. No weapon or instrument was found near her by which the wound could have been inflicted. An inquest was held yesterday afternoon but the particulars have not transpired.

## Saturday 26 January 1833
CLIFTON MURDER – On Thursday last another investigation into this mysterious affair took place before Sir George Armytage, Bart. at the house of Mr Samuel Middleham, Armytage Arms, Clifton, and after a tedious enquiry, the evidence in many instances varying from the depositions given before the coroner, we are sorry that no clue has been found to the perpetrators. A reward of £100 is offered in another part of our paper.

## ONE HUNDRED POUNDS REWARD
Whereas at some Period betwixt NINE o'Clock on Monday Night the 31st of December last, and THREE o'Clock in the afternoon on Tuesday the First of January instant, ELIZABETH RAYNER, late

of Clifton upon Calder was cruelly MURDERED in CLIFTON WOOD, by having her Throat cut by some Person or Persons unknown.

ONE HUNDRED POUNDS is offered and will be paid by the Constable of Clifton to any Person or Persons who will give information to *Sir George Armitage, Baronet,* of the Perpetrator or Perpetrators of this horrid Deed, so that he, she or they may be Convicted of the said Offence. And if an Accomplice therein will give such information so that the real Offender may be brought to Justice, he or she shall receive the said Reward and an Application will be made to his Majesty to grant his

ROYAL PARDON
except to the Person who really committed the Deed.
CHARLES RAMSDEN, Constable of Clifton
Clifton, 14th January, 1833

**Saturday 23 February 1833**
THE LATE MURDER IN CLIFTON WOOD
A reward of £200 has been offered for the apprehension of the murderers of Elizabeth Rayner, who was found dead in Clifton Wood, in the West Riding, and his Majesty's most gracious pardon to any person concerned, except the actual perpetrator of the deed) who shall give some information as may lead to the conviction of the offenders.

# Charles Ramsden's obituary

8 August 1893

Death of Mr Charles Ramsden. It is with sincere regret that we have to record the death of so well known a resident as Mr Charles Ramsden, a publican and farmer, whose demise took place last Tuesday at 12.30 noon. Deceased had been somewhat unwell during the past two years, as a result of a severe attack of influenza which he had when that malady was so prevalent a couple of years ago. Medical aid had very often to be called in during that period. On Friday the 28th ult., Mr Ramsden had a very bad attack of illness, but he had apparently got well over it last week, and was out of doors so late as last Friday, and although he was somewhat poorly on the Sunday, yet he was able to sit in the room with a few friends in the evening. On Monday, however, deceased gradually grew worse and was unable to leave his bed, and although the best medical attention was paid him and despite every attention and careful nursing, deceased passed away as above stated. Charles Ramsden was one of the best known residents in Clifton and not only was he a familiar face in his own village, but for many miles round. He was born on the 18th June 1833 and consequently seen 60 summers. At the time of his birth, Mr Ramsden's father resided at the bottom of Clifton, and there carried on the business of a leather currier in a building opposite the present Black Horse Inn. Thomas and Ann Ramsden, the parents of the deceased, both belonged to very old local families and they successfully carried on the business of leather curriers until 1869. Ann Ramsden died in that year, having survived her husband a few years. She was a shrewd businesswoman, and many of the older generation of traders in the Spen Valley retain lively recollections of her business capabilities during the years which followed her husband's death. The son, Charles Ramsden, entered into the occupancy of the Armytage Arms in 1861, and took over the farm attached to the house. The house itself was very largely renovated just previously, additions also being made. Mr Ramsden still kept on the leather currying business in conjunction with his brother (who died in 1874) the business being relinquished in 1886. At the Armytage Arms deceased speedily began to make the house a centre of attraction. In 1868 he laid the bowling green, which was afterwards taken over by Clifton Subscription Bowling Club. A cricket green was also laid in the field adjoining the farm yard and very soon the house became a familiar place to residents for miles around. As a farmer Mr Ramsden was very fond of horses and horse breeding. Only recently he rented an addition to the Armytage Arms farm and at the time of his death he was the largest farmer on the Kirklees Estate, over 200 acres being included in his farm. During the past 20 years Mr Ramsden was intimately connected with the Clifton Highway Surveyors and was last a member of the board in 1892. As a caterer for public parties he had, along with his respected widow, gained great esteem from thousands of locals who have at various times partaken of the good fare provided by the host and hostess of the Armytage Arms. He was of genial disposition and his removal from amongst us will be keenly felt by all with whom he had come in contact. Deceased leaves a widow, three sons and four daughters. The interment is to take place at St. John's Clifton at twelve noon today.

# References

## Books and Magazines

*The Making of the English Working Class*, E.P. Thompson

*The Story of the Ancient Parish of Hartshead- cum-Clifton*, H.N. and M. Pobjoy

*I Didn't Know That: Glimpses of the History of Clifton, a West Yorkshire Village*, Margaret Sharp

'Old Occupations: The Currier', S. Drummond, *Family Tree* magazine, September 1995, volume 11

'Apprenticeships', Lisa Spurrier, *Berkshire Family Historian*

## Websites

www.met. police.uk

www.ancestry.com

www.revolutionaryplayers.org.uk

www.timeanddate.com/calendar/year= 1833mdlp.co.uk/resources/general/poor_law

www.derbyshire-peakdistict.co.uk/hathersage

www.genuki.org.uk

www.crutchleyhistory.co.uk

www.lowercalderlegends.wordpress.com

www.measuringworth.com/ukcompare

http://freepages.history.rootsweb.ancestry.
com/~calderdalecompanion/

## ORGANISATIONS

Calderdale Family History Society

Huddersfield and District Family History Society

Yorkshire Archaeological Society

Halifax Antiquarian Society

## DOCUMENTS

Censuses

Parish records: St Peter's, Hartshead, St Mary's, Elland, All Saints', Dewsbury

Pigot's Trade Directory: Yorkshire, 1828–29

History, Directory and Gazetteer of Yorkshire, Volume 1: West Riding, 1822

Hartshead Vestry Minutes, 1819–39

## NEWSPAPERS

*Halifax Guardian and Huddersfield and Bradford Advertiser*

*Brighouse and Elland Echo*

*Halifax Courier*

*Halifax Guardian*

# Chapter title sources

1   Thou dirge of the dying year: Shelley, 'Ode to the West Wind'

2   A branch of one of your antediluvian families: William
    Congreve, *Love for Love*

3   See how love and murder will out: William Congreve,
    *Love for Love*

4   Murder most foul: Shakespeare, *Hamlet*

5   She feared no danger: Dryden: 'The Hind and the Panther'

6   A little one-eyed blinking sort of place: Thomas Hardy, *Tess
    of the Durbervilles*

7   A policeman's lot is not a happy one: W.S. Gilbert, *The Pirates
    of Penzance*

8   We are family: Edwards and Rodgers, 'We Are Family',
    recorded by Sister Sledge

9   Pitched past pitch of grief: Gerard Manley Hopkins,
    'No Worst there is None'

10  When lovely woman stoops to folly, and finds too late that
    men betray: Goldsmith: *The Vicar of Wakefield*

11     Men love in haste, but they detest at leisure: Lord Byron, 'Don Juan'

12     T'ain't what you say, it's the way that you say it: Melvin 'Sy' Oliver & James 'Trummy' Young, 'T'ain't what you do'

13     It is a wise father that knows its child: William Shakespeare, *Merchant of Venice*

14     It is difficult suddenly to put aside a long-standing love: it is difficult, but somehow you must do it: Catullus, 'Carmina'

15     The man's desire is for the woman: the woman's desire is rarely other than for the desire of the man: S.T. Coleridge: *Table Talk*

16     Let me tell you about the very rich. They are different to you and me: F. Scott Fitzgerald, *All the Sad Young Men*

17     Because I could not stop for Death, he kindly stopped for me: Emily Dickinson, 'The Chariot'

18     And we forget because we must, and not because we will: Matthew Arnold, 'Absence'

19     Fears and fancies thick upon me come: William Wordsworth, 'The Redbreast Chasing the Butterfly'

20     I'm following in Father's footsteps: E.W. Rogers, music hall song

21     And with thee fade into the forest dim: John Keats, 'Ode to a Nightingale'

# Illustrations

001 Baptismal entry for Elizabeth Rayner with the Reverend Patrick Brontë's signature. (Parish register of St Peter's, Hartshead, courtesy of Wakefield Archives)

002 Baptismal font in use at the time of Elizabeth's baptism. (Author)

003 Detail of the old altar with Armytage family coat of arms. (Author)

004 St Peter's, Hartshead (Dan Ambler)

005 Man drawing wire, turn of century. (By kind permission of Warrington Museum and Art Gallery)

006 Well Lane, Clifton, where the Rayner family lived. (Drawing by Albert T. Pile for *Brighouse and Elland Echo*, 18 August 1950, courtesy of the *Brighouse Echo*)

007 Black Horse Inn, Clifton, 2010. (Author)

008 Looking down Westgate towards Clifton Wood and Sheep Cote Lane. (Author)

009 Sheep Cote Lane, Clifton. (Author)

010 Footpath towards estate gate into wood. (Dan Ambler)

Lightning Source UK Ltd.
Milton Keynes UK
171855UK00001B/4/P